ALLSENSORS 2019

The Fourth International Conference on Advances in Sensors, Actuators, Metering and Sensing

February 24 – 28, 2019

Athens, Greece

ALLSENSORS 2019 Editors

Paulo E. Cruvinel, Embrapa Instrumentation, Brazil
Antonio Valente, INESC TEC - INESC Technology and Science and University of Trás-os-Montes and Alto Douro, Vila Real, Portugal

Printed from e-media with permission by:

Curran Associates, Inc.
57 Morehouse Lane
Red Hook, NY 12571

CURRAN ASSOCIATES INC. proceedings .com

Some format issues inherent in the e-media version may also appear in this print version.

Printed by Curran Associates, Inc. (2019)

International Academy, Research, and Industry Association (IARIA)
412 Derby Way
Wilmington, DE 19810

Phone: (408) 893-6407
Fax: (408) 527-6351

petre@iaria.org

Additional copies of this publication are available from:

Curran Associates, Inc.
57 Morehouse Lane
Red Hook, NY 12571 USA
Phone: 845-758-0400
Fax: 845-758-2633
Email: curran@proceedings.com
Web: www.proceedings.com

Table of Contents

ALLSENSORS 2019

Forward

The Fourth International Conference on Advances in Sensors, Actuators, Metering and Sensing (ALLSENSORS 2019), held in Athens, Greece, February 24 - 28, 2019, covered related topics on theory practice and applications of sensor devices, techniques, data acquisition and processing, and on wired and wireless sensors and sensor networks.

Sensor networks and sensor-based systems support many applications today above ground. Underwater operations and applications are quite limited by comparison. Most applications refer to remotely controlled submersibles and wide-area data collection systems at a coarse granularity. Other remote sensing domains and applications are using special sensing devices and services. Transducers and actuators complement the monitoring and control and constitute an area of interest related to sensors. They make use of specific sensor-based measurements and convey appropriate control actions.

ALLSENSORS 2019 was intended to serve as a forum for researchers from the academia and the industry, professionals, standard developers, policy makers, investors and practitioners to present their recent results, to exchange ideas, and to establish new partnerships and collaborations.

The accepted papers covered a large spectrum of topics on techniques and applications, best practices, awareness and experiences as well as future trends and needs (both in research and practice) related to all aspects of sensor-based applications and services.

We take here the opportunity to warmly thank all the members of the ALLSENSORS 2019 technical program committee as well as the numerous reviewers. The creation of such a broad and high quality conference program would not have been possible without their involvement. We also kindly thank all the authors that dedicated much of their time and efforts to contribute to the ALLSENSORS 2019. We truly believe that thanks to all these efforts, the final conference program consists of top quality contributions.

This event could also not have been a reality without the support of many individuals, organizations and sponsors. In addition, we also gratefully thank the members of the ALLSENSORS 2019 organizing committee for their help in handling the logistics and for their work that is making this professional meeting a success.

We hope the ALLSENSORS 2019 was a successful international forum for the exchange of ideas and results between academia and industry and to promote further progress on the topics of sensors.

We also hope that Athens provided a pleasant environment during the conference and everyone saved some time for exploring this beautiful city.

ALLSENSORS 2019 Chairs

ALLSENSORS Steering Committee

ALLSENSORS Industry/Research Advisory Committee

ALLSENSORS 2019

COMMITTEE

ALLSENSORS Steering Committee

Sergey Yurish, Excelera, S. L. | IFSA, Spain
Michael Niedermayer, Beuth University of Applied Sciences - Berlin, Germany
Jagannathan Sarangapani, Missouri University of Science and Technology, USA
Qingsong Xu, University of Macau, Macau, China
Càndid Reig, University of Valencia, Spain
Sandrine Bernardini, Aix Marseille University, France
Gholamreza Alirezaei, Institute for Theoretical Information Technology | RWTH Aachen University, Germany
Tamer Nadeem, Old Dominion University, USA

ALLSENSORS Industry/Research Advisory Committee

Paulo E. Cruvinel, Embrapa Instrumentation, Brazil
Yuriy S. Shmaliy, Universidad de Guanajuato, Mexico
Suzanne Lesecq, LIALP - Commissariat à l'énergie atomique et aux énergies alternatives MINATEC Campus, France
Xin Wang, Qualcomm, Inc., USA
Matteo Tonezzer, Italian National Research Council - Institute of Materials for Electronics and Magnetism (CNR - IMEM), Italy

ALLSENSORS 2019 Technical Program Committee

Francesco Aggogeri, University of Brescia, Italy
Vahid Akbari, UiT The Arctic University of Norway, Norway
Amin Al-Habaibeh, Nottingham Trent University, UK
Giovanni Albani, Istituto Auxologico Italiano - IRCCS, Italy
Falah H. Ali, University of Sussex, UK
Ferri M. H. Aliabadi, Imperial College London, UK
Parastoo Alinia, Washington State University, USA
Gholamreza Alirezaei, Institute for Theoretical Information Technology | RWTH Aachen University, Germany
Darius Andriukaitis, Kaunas University of Technology, Lithuania
Anett Bailleu, Hochschule für Technik und Wirtschaft Berlin, Germany
Roberto Beghi, Università degli Studi di Milano, Italy
Roc Berenguer, Tecnun - University of Navarra, Spain
Sandrine Bernardini, Aix Marseille University, France
Partha Bhattacharyya, Indian Institute of Engineering Science and Technology (IIEST), India
Xavier Boddaert, Microelectronic Center in Provence - Ecole Nationale Supérieure des Mines de St Etienne, France
Ismail Butun, Abdullah Gul University, Kayseri, Turkey
Mauro Callejas Cuervo, Universidad Pedagógica y Tecnológica de Colombia, Colombia
Hung Cao, UC Irvine, USA
Juan-Vicente Capella-Hernández, Universitat Politècnica de València, Spain

Vítor Carvalho, IPCA-EST-2Ai Lab & Algoritmi Research Center, Portugal
Paula María Castro Castro, Universidade da Coruña, Spain
Nunzio Cennamo, University of Campania Luigi Vanvitelli, Italy
Debashish Chakravarty, Indian Institute of Technology Kharagpur, India
Omar Cheikhrouhou, Taif University, KSA
Nan-Fu Chiu, National Taiwan Normal University, Taiwan
Sung Ho Cho, Hanyang University, Korea
Adriano Cola, CNR- IMM (National Council of Research - Institute of Microelectronics and Microsystems), Italy
Paulo E. Cruvinel, Embrapa Instrumentation, Brazil
Antonio Eduardo de Barros Ruano, University of Algarve, Portugal
Danilo De Rossi, University of Pisa, Italy
Paulo de Souza, Data61 | CSIRO, Australia
Michele Dei, Institut de Microelectrònica de Barcelona - Centro Nacional de Microelectrónica IMB-CNM(CSIC), Spain
Huazeng Deng, University of Washington, Seattle, USA
Madhavrao K. Deore, Arts, Science and Commerce College, Ozar (Mig), India
Emiliano Descrovi, Politecnico di Torino, Italy
Chérif Diallo, Université Gaston Berger, Senegal
Mauro Dragone, Heriot-Watt University | Edinburgh Center for Robotics, UK
Surya Durbha, CSRE - IIT Bombay, India
M. Emre Erdem, Istanbul Bilgi University, Turkey
Javad Foroughi, University of Wollongong, Australia
Attilio Frangi, Politecnico di Milano, Italy
Orlando Frazão, INESCTEC Porto, Portugal
Kelum Gamage, Glasgow University, UK
Félix J. García Clemente, University of Murcia, Spain
Valentina Giovenzana, Università degli Studi di Milano, Italy
Jesus Manuel Gómez de Gabriel, Universidad de Málaga, Spain
Raffaele Gravina, University of Calabria, Italy
Yigang He, Hefei University of Technology, China
Candelaria Hernandez Goya, Universidad de La Laguna, Spain
Hans Peter Herzig, Ecole Polytechnique Fédérale de Lausanne (EPFL), Switzerland
Daniel Hill, The Institute for Molecular Science (ICMol) - Universitat de Valencia, Spain
Carmen Horrillo, ITEFI-CSIC, Madrid, Spain
Wei Min Huang, Nanyang Technological University, Singapore
Yanqiu Huang, University of Bremen, Germany
Rui Igreja, Universidade NOVA de Lisboa, Portugal
Md. Rajibul Islam, University of Malaya, Malaysia
Ahmed Abu Ismaiel, Municipality of Abasan Al-Kabira, Gaza, Palestine
Emmanuel Iwuoha, University of Western Cape, South Africa
Rajan Jha, Indian Institute of Technology Bhubaneswar, India
Zhiyu Jiang, University of Chinese Academy of Sciences, China
Anand Y. Joshi, G. H. Patel College of Engineering & Technology, Gujarat, India
Taeho Jung, Illinois Institute of Technology, USA
Grigoris Kaltsas, Technological Educational Institute (T.E.I) of Athens, Greece
Latifah Munirah Kamarudin, Universiti Malaysia Perlis, Malaysia
Amarjeet Kaur, University of Delhi, India

Aghiad Khadour, IFSTTAR - French Institute of Science and Technology for Transport, Spatial Planning, Development and Networks, France
Unmesh Khati, Indian Institute of Technology Bombay, India
Roman Kolcun, Imperial College London, UK
M. Bala Krishna, USICT, Guru Gobind Singh Indraprastha University, India
Jan Kubicek, VSB-Technical University of Ostrava, Czech Republic
Gabriela Kuncova, Institute of Chemical Process Fundamentals of the ASCR, Czech Republic
Sophie LaRochelle, Center for Optics, Photonics and Lasers (COPL) - Université Laval, Canada
Seongsoo Lee, Soongsil University, Korea
Maria Lepore, Università della Campania "Luigi Vanvitelli", Italy
Suzanne Lesecq, LIALP - Commissariat à l'énergie atomique et aux énergies alternatives MINATEC Campus, France
Jingbin Liu, Wuhan University, China
Yu-Lung Lo, National Cheng Kung University (NCKU), Taiwan
Wen Shiung Lour, National Taiwan Ocean University, Taiwan
Antonio Loureiro, Universidade Federal de Minas Gerais, Brazil
Jian Lu, National Institute of Advanced Industrial Science and Technology (AIST), Japan
Vladimir Lukin, National Aerospace University, Kharkov, Ukraine
Dandan Ma, University of Chinese Academy of Sciences, China
Yufei Ma, Harbin Institute of Technology, China
Stephane Maag, Télécom SudParis, France
Monika Maciejewska, Wroclaw University of Science and Technology, Poland
Marco Manso, PARTICLE | SME, Portugal
Vincenzo Marletta, DIEEI - University of Catania, Italy
Rodrigo Martins, New University of Lisbon, Portugal
Bodh Raj Mehta, Indian Institute of Technology Delhi, India
Marek Miskowicz, AGH University of Science and Technology, Poland
Tamer Nadeem, Old Dominion University, USA
Dan Necsulescu, University of Ottawa, Canada
Michael Niedermayer, Beuth University of Applied Sciences - Berlin, Germany
Brendan O'Flynn, Tyndall National Institute, Ireland
Michael O'Grady, University College Dublin, Ireland
Vladimir Ogourtsov, Tyndall National Institute - University College Cork, Ireland
Min-Chun Pan, National Central University (NCU), Taiwan
Devidas Ramrao Patil, Rani Laxmibai Mahavidyalaya Parola, Jalgaon, India
Luigi Patrono, University of Salento, Italy
Pablo Pérez García, University of Seville / Institute of Microelectronics in Seville, Spain
Salvatore Petralia, STMicroelectronics, Catania, Italy
Manh-Huong Phan, University of South Florida, USA
Francesc Pozo, Escola d'Enginyeria de Barcelona Est (EEBE) | Universitat Politècnica de Catalunya (UPC), Spain
Rajinikumar Ramalingam, Karlsruhe Institute for Technology, Germany
Reza Rashidi, State University of New York - Alfred State College, USA
Càndid Reig, University of Valencia, Spain
Almudena Rivadeneyra, University of Granada, Spain
Christos Riziotis, National Hellenic Research Foundation, Greece
Bahram Djafari Rouhani, Université de Lille 1 Sciences et Technologies, France
Adolfo H. Ruelas Puente, Universidad Autonoma de Baja California, Mexico

Giovanni Saggio, University of Rome "Tor Vergata", Italy
Amgad A. Salama, Alexandria University, Egypt
Jagannathan (Jag) Sarangapani, Missouri University of Science and Technology, USA
Marco Scaioni, Politecnico di Milano, Italy
Emiliano Schena, Università Campus Bio-Medico di Roma, Italy
Leonello Servoli, Istituto Nazionale di Fisica Nucleare, Perugia, Italy
Yuriy S. Shmaliy, Universidad de Guanajuato, Mexico
Marius Silaghi, Florida Institute of Technology, USA
Cristian Stanciu, University Politehnica of Bucharest, Romania
Mu-Chun Su, National Central University, Taiwan
Andrzej Szczurek, Wroclaw University of Science and Technology, Poland
Roman Szewczyk, Warsaw University of Technology, Poland
Ryszard Tadeusiewicz, AGH University of Science and Technology, Krakow, Poland
Pedro Renato Tavares Pinho, ISEL / Instituto de Telecomunicações, Portugal
Alessandro Tognetti, Research Center "E. Piaggio" | University of Pisa, Italy
Kiyoshi Toko, Kyushu University, Japan
Matteo Tonezzer, Italian National Research Council - Institute of Materials for Electronics and Magnetism (CNR - IMEM), Italy
Fernando Torres Medina, University of Alicante, Spain
Daniele Tosi, Nazarbayev University, Kazakhstan
Federico Tramarin, University of Padova, Italy
Carlos M. Travieso-González, University of Las Palmas de Gran Canaria, Spain
Pere Tuset-Peiró, Universitat Oberta de Catalunya, Spain
Antonio Valente, UTAD University / INESC TEC - INESC Technology and Science, Portugal
Periasamy Vengadesh, University of Malaya, Malaysia
Sudip Vhaduri, IBM Research, Zurich, Switzerland
Pedro Viana Baptista, Universidade NOVA de Lisboa, Portugal
Xin Wang, Qualcomm Inc, USA
Magnus Willander, Linköping University, Sweden
Qiong Wu, University of Texas at Arlington, USA
Qingsong Xu, University of Macau, China
Zhengwei Yang, Zhengwei Yang, United States Department of Agriculture / George Mason University, USA
Murat Kaya Yapici, Sabanci University, Istanbul, Turkey
Nicolas H. Younan, Mississippi State University, USA
Yanguang (Sunny) Yu, University of Wollongong, Australia
Sergey Yurish, Excelera, S. L. | IFSA, Spain
Bernhard Zagar, Institute for Measurement Technology | Johannes Kepler University Linz, Austria
Ammar Zakaria, Universiti Malaysia Perlis, Malaysia
Lan Zhang, National Institute of Advanced Industrial Science and Technology (AIST), Japan
Pengfei Zhang, Nanyang Technological University, Singapore
Zonghua Zhang, Hebei University of Technology, China
Jianhua Zhou, Sun Yat-Sen University, China
Xiaohong Zhou, Tsinghua University, China
Zeljko Zilic, McGill University, Canada
Mohd Zamani Zulkifli, Photonics Research Centre | University of Malaya, Malaysia

Research on the Performance of Solid-State pH Sensor Affected by the Sensing Materials

Lan Zhang, Jian Lu, Ryutaro Maeda
Research Center for Ubiquitous MEMS and Micro Engineering (UMEMSME)
National Institute of Advanced Industrial Science and Technology (AIST)
Tsukuba, Japan
email: chou-ran@aist.go.jp,
email:jian-lu@aist.go.jp
email:maeda-ryutaro@aist.go.jp

Hirofumi Nogami
Department of Mechanical Engineering
Kyushu University
Fukuoka, Japan
email: nogami.hirofumi.406@m.kyushu-u.ac.jp

Abstract— **We developed a solid pH sensor, which can implement a real-time monitoring of pH value with low power consumption and high accuracy. In this work, three kinds of different metal oxide materials are used to fabricate the sensing electrode layers. Mechanical and functional properties comparisons are of material coatings on the sensor electrodes are comprehensively evaluated. As the results show, the given pH sensor based on SnO_2 can keep a linear output proportional to the changes in the pH value and has a higher sensitivity of >530 μV/pH.**

Keywords- pH value test; solid state; MEMS process; Metal Oxide

I. Introduction and Electrode Fabrication

Measurements of pH are important in many fields, such as chemical engineering, medicine, environmental science, agriculture, and many other applications. Recently, Micro-electromechanical systems (MEMS) technology has undergone many advances, such as super compact size, high sensitivity and high uniformity of working functions. As part of the MEMS researchers, we would like to contribute to the industrial revolution and improve the pH measurement technology.

Recently, a solid-type pH sensor has been developed for real-time pH measurement. The given solid pH sensor offers the advantages of field effect transistor and metal oxide sensing techniques. The sensor system can be fabricated in a compact size by eliminating the reference solution. The solid-state sensor structure is fit for long-term pH measurement, and the separate sensing electrode can be patterned with a suitable capture structure for various test environments. In previous research works, the given indium tin oxide (ITO)-based solid-type pH sensor was used to test the pH value of Japanese cows' stomach for monitoring the health condition of them. The ITO-sensor can keep a good linear output in the testing range from pH 4.5-8.0. The given sensor can test the pH value in cows' stomach well [1].

However, for realizing a trillion-sensor society, i.e., arbitrary distributing of the sensor node in diverse testing environment, the solid-state pH sensor needs a larger working range, higher sensitivity and longer durability. Thus, in this work, different sensing materials are used to fabricate the sensor electrode. Mechanical and functional properties comparisons are of material coatings on the electrodes are comprehensively evaluated.

Figure 1 shows the schematic view of our proposed pH sensor measurement system with potential application fields. MEMS fabrication technology was used in this work to realize the sensing electrode with high dimensional and performance homogeneity. The given typical pH sensor prototype combines the functional components of sensor electrodes, measurement units and transmission boards. A metal-oxide-sensing electrode connects the gate terminal of a MOSFET, the specific FET was loaded on the testing board was used to measure the pH value of target solutions. Transmission board has a CPU, a wireless module and a chip thermometer unit to coding and transmitting the tested date, recording the environment temperature for calibration, respectively.

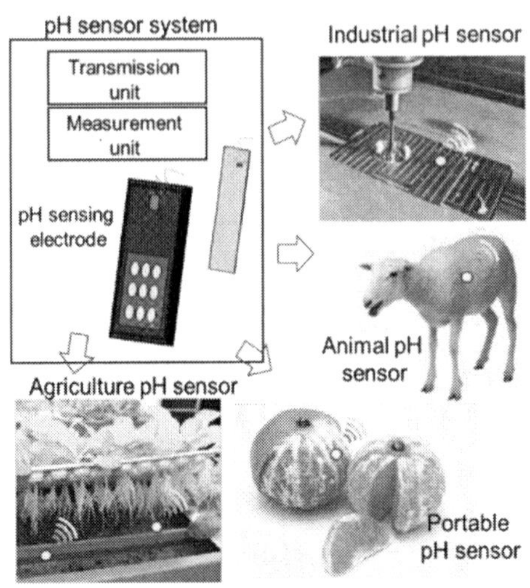

Figure 1. Schematic view of our proposed pH sensor measurement system with potential application fields.

The fabrication procedure of the pH sensor electrodes has been introduced comprehensively in our previous works [2]. By the MEMS technique, 47 die chip sensor electrodes can be fabricated on a 4-inch silicon wafer. The flat area of every single electrode can be controlled at <120 mm^2. The die chip of sensor electrodes was fabricated with a compact size can induce the packaged sensor system enjoying a high flexible application potential in feature works.

II. PRELIMINARY MEASUREMENT RESULTS

A. Mechanical properties comparisons are of sensing materials coatings

Figure 2 shows the measured surface roughness of different sensing materials with arithmetical average value (Ra). The insets are AFM scanning images on the sensing electrode local area. The AFM images showed the surface topographies of fabricated Ta_2O_5, SnO_2 and ITO with the arithmetical average roughness value of 2.5 nm, 1.2 nm and 1.1 nm, respectively. As the AFM image shows, the sensing films on the electrode retained a smooth surface with less morphological defects after the MEMS etching processes. The sensing electrode enjoys uniform surface and is very suitable for use in the development of an electronic device, because, in some cases, the sensing film has a rough grain surface, which can completely obscure the material intrinsic charge transport properties.

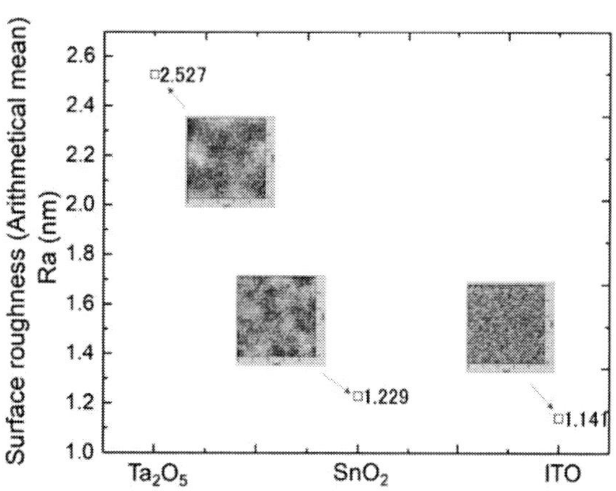

Figure 2. Measured arithmetical average surface roughness of different sensing materials. The insets are the AFM images of the sensing electrode local area.

TABLE I. THE COMPARISON OF SENSING MATERIALS

	Ta_2O_5	SnO_2	ITO
Fabrication	Etching	Etching	Lift-off or etching
pH range	2-11	3-10	4-9
Surface homogeneity	2.527 nm (Ra)	1.229 nm (Ra)	1.141 nm (Ra)
Drift	>pH0.1	pH0.05	±pH0.1

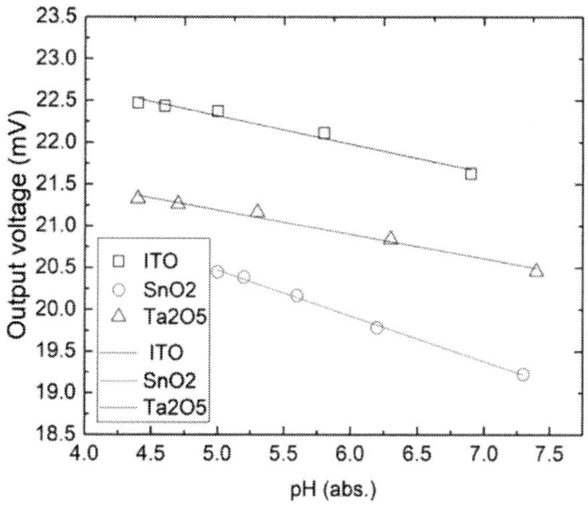

Figure 3. The output voltage of pH sensor with different sensing martials against the measured pH values.

B. Functional properties comparison of sensing metrials coatings

Figure 3 shows the output voltage of pH sensor with different sensing martials versus the measured pH values. As the results show, the ITO-based and Ta_2O_5-based pH sensors have the sensitivities of 340 μV/pH and 290 μV/pH, respectively. The given pH sensor based on SnO_2 can keep a linear output proportional to the changes in the pH value and has a higher sensitivity of 530 μV/pH. Table 1 shows the comparison between the sensing materials. We can understand the merits and demerits of given materials, reasonably. More detailed results and discussion will be presented at the conference.

III. DISCUSSIION AND CONCLUSION

We developed a solid-state pH sensor for real time pH monitoring. Different sensing materials are used to fabricated the sensor electrode. Mechanical and functional properties comparisons are of material coatings on the electrodes are comprehensively evaluated. The solid-state sensor can be packaged super compact size as a portable sensor device to test water, foods and fruits in our daily life. Moreover, in industrial field, many low-cost solid pH sensors can provide mass data of target solutions and water to help the company realizing an Internet of Things management system.

REFERENCES

[1] L. Zhang, J. Lu, H. Okada, H. Nogami, T. Itoh, and S. Arai, "Low-Power Highly Sensitive pH sensor with μ-dots protective structures for monitoring rumen in cows in real-time," IEEE Sens. J. vol. 17, pp. 7281 - 7289, 2017.

[2] L. Zhang, J. Lu, H. Okada, H. Nogami, and T. Itoh, "Development of ITO- and FET-based cow rumen sensor for long-term pH value monitoring," Symposium on Design, Test, Integration and Packaging of MEMS/MOEMS (DTIP), vol. 2016, pp.92-96, May 2016.

Textile Chemiresistors for Gas Detection – New Materials of Sensitive Layers

Martin Vrňata, Eva Marešová, Jan Vlček, Přemysl Fitl, David Tomeček
Department of Physics and Measurements
University of Chemistry and Technology Prague
Prague, Czech Republic
e-mail: martin.vrnata@vscht.cz

Michal Novotný
Physical Institute
The Czech Academy of Sciences
Prague, Czech Republic
e-mail: novotnym@fzu.cz

***Abstract*—The contribution presents novel research of textile chemiresistors prepared on textile substrates (Evolon and Polyester) equipped with graphite electrodes and sensitive layers based on polymer ionic liquid. The polymer ionic liquid, i.e. poly(tributylhexylphosphonium 3-sulfopropylacrylate) was in-situ polymerized on the textile substrates. The responses of such sensors to toxic gases (10 ppm of methanol, nitrogen dioxide, 4-bromoacetophenone and diethylmalonate) were then investigated in dc-mode of measurement – the reference was "pure" synthetic air. It was shown that sensor dynamics depends mainly on molecular weight of the analytes.**

Keywords-chemiresistor; textile substrate; polymer ionic liquids; detection of toxic gases.

I. INTRODUCTION

Application of functional elements and nanostructures on flexible substrates is a promising trend in electronics. Also for fabrication of chemiresistors, there are intensively studied substrates, such as plastic foil, paper and fabric; they seem to be a suitable alternative for conventional "hard" alumina substrates equipped with metal electrodes. Textiles are materials with great potential, whose mechanical properties (high strength, large surface area, lightness, flexibility, effortless integration into clothing) make it unique even in comparison with other flexible substrates [1]. There are several ways to add new functionalities to textiles when used in sensor applications. The textile substrate can be covered with gas sensitive layer by "wet" and "vacuum" coating techniques, e.g., ink-jet printing or magnetron sputtering technology. A common feature of textile sensors is that they operate at either laboratory or at a slightly higher temperature. Therefore, organic conductors are preferred to be their sensitive layers.

Polymerized ionic liquids (PILs) have been reported for the first time in 1998, and a brief overview of their properties can be found, e.g. in [2]. Their electrotransport properties are unique (when compared with other organic substances), as they are purely ionic conductors. Moreover, majority of them can be considered as single-ion conductors. PILs are characterized by large capacity to absorb analytes with small molecules – especially CO_2 and water. After such absorption, the internal volume of polymer is modified, hence the mobility of ions changes. Such a phenomenon could work as a prospective transducer mechanism in chemiresistors. This property of PILs is very valuable, because namely CO_2 and numerous other analytes (whose molecule has neither redox properties, nor dipole moments) cannot be detected on chemiresistors by any other mechanism.

II. EXPERIMENTAL

This contribution details the development of a gas sensing chemiresistor using a non-conductive textile (dimensions 10 x 15 mm) as the substrate. The architecture of the sensor can be seen in Figure 1. Two kinds of textiles of different composition and method of production were used: Evolon - non-woven textile (70% polyester/30% polyamide) and Polyester. These textiles were first continuously cleaned in methanol using Soxhlet extraction (10 cycles) then washed with deionized water and finally dried at room temperature. In order to improve the mechanical flexibility of the sensor, the thermal adhesive film (Sealon Co., Ltd.) was laminated on the back side of the textile. The film was applied via a Heated Roll Laminator (model Titan-110) under the following conditions: adhesive bonding temperature of 80°C for 10 s, at a pressure between 70-140 kPa.

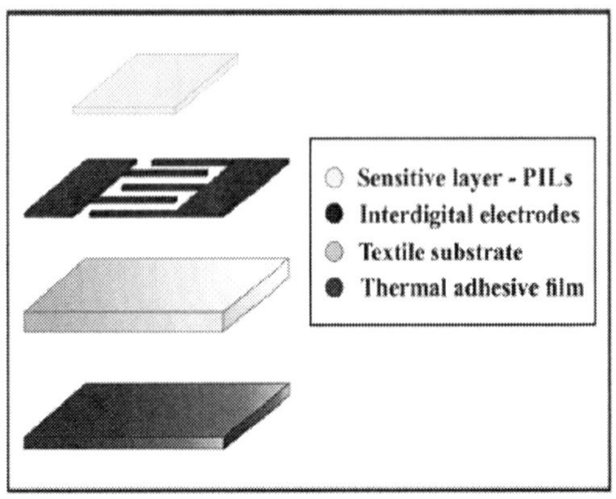

Figure 1. Vertical architecture of the textile-based sensor (left) and its real appearance indicating variable distances between electrodes (right).

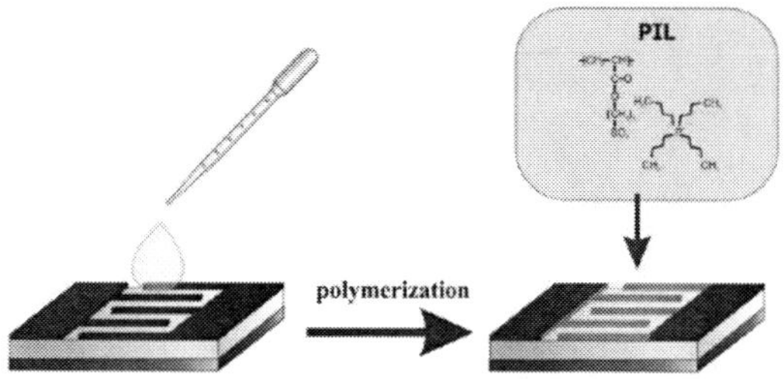

Figure 2. The deposition of sensitive layer on textile substrate.

The gas sensitive layer is composed of the following polymer ionic liquid: poly(tributylhexylphosphonium 3-sulfopropylacrylate) abbreviated as $P_{4,4,4,6}SPA$.

In the next step, the polymerization mixture was prepared, having the following composition: $P_{4,4,4,6}SPA$ monomer, photoinitiator (phenylbis (2,4,6-trimethylbenzoyl) phosphine oxide) and crosslinker (trimethylolpropane ethoxylate triacrylate) dissolved in the solvent mixture (deionized water with acetonitrile). This mixture was photo-polymerized directly onto the surface of the textile substrate. Firstly, the mixture was drop-cast onto the surface of the textile using a micropipette and subsequently it was polymerized using a LMI-6000 Fiber-Lite white light source (~200 kLux) for 30 min to create compact sensitive film on textile substrate. The process is schematically depicted in Figure 2.

The dc-responses of the prepared sensors were evaluated according to (1):

$$S_{dc} = R_{air} / R_{gas}. \qquad (1)$$

The symbol S_{dc} denotes dc-response, R_{air} steady-state resistance value of the sensor in synthetic air and R_{gas} steady-state resistance value of the sensor in detected analyte.

III. Results and Conclusions

Just a few examples: As for dependence of sensor response on concentration of the analyte, an example is given on Figure 3, which illustrates detection of methanol (MeOH) on sensor based on $P_{4,4,4,6}$SPA. The grey areas correspond to reference atmosphere – synthetic air, the white areas to synthetic air with MeOH vapor. What is apparent: (i) the sensor baseline (R_{air}) slightly drifts to lower values; (ii) an average value of S_{dc} achieves 1.05 for 100 ppb, 1.25 for 1 ppm, 1.29 for 10 ppm and 1.39 for 100 ppm of MeOH, respectively; (iii) the sensor output signal exhibits a very low level of noise, hence as low concentration as 100 ppb of MeOH is above the detection limit.

Figure 4 presents dynamic response of $P_{4,4,4,6}$SPA sensor to 10 ppm of yperite. The meaning of grey/white areas is the same as in the previous figure.

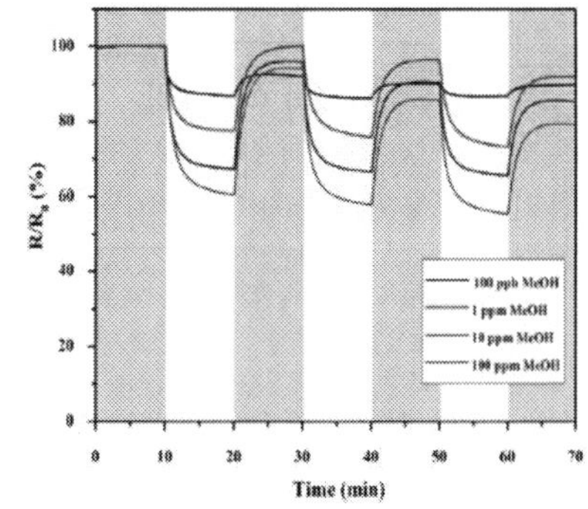

Figure 3. Response of sensor with $P_{4,4,4,6}$SPA to

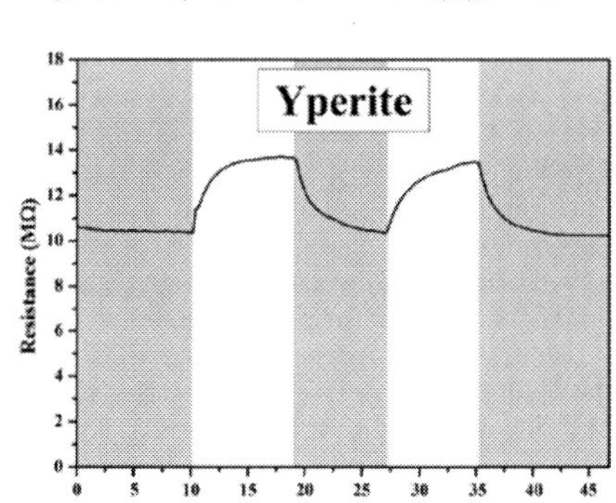

Figure 4. Response of sensor with $P_{4,4,4,6}$SPA to 10 ppm of yperite.

As for response dynamics: It is apparent that both the response- and recovery- time is approximately 5 min when detecting yperite and the response dynamics for yperite is (in general) slower than that for MeOH.

The only chemiresistor based on PILs was reported in [3]. It has $R_{air} \approx 1.7$ GΩ, i.e. 2-3 orders higher than our samples. Such high baseline brings troubles in practical operation.

Acknowledgment

This work was supported by COST Action CA15107: Multi-Functional Nano-Carbon Composite Materials Network (MultiComp), project id.code and title: LTC17 Nano-Carbon Composite Materials for Thin Film Chemical Gas Sensors and Photovoltaics.

References

[1] L. M. Castano and A. B. Flatau, "Smart Fabric Sensors and e-textiles Technologies: A Review", Smart Materials and Structures, vol. 23, art. no. 053001, pp. 1-27, 2014, doi: 10.1088/0964-1726/23/5/053001.

[2] N. Nishimura and H. Ohno, "15th Anniversary of Polymerized Ionic Liquids", Polymer, vol. 55, pp. 3289-3297, 2014, doi: 10.1016/j.polymer.2014.02.042.

[3] C. Willa and D. Koziej, "When Nanoparticles Meet Poly(Ionic Liquid)s: Chemoresitive CO_2 Sensing at Room Temperature", Advanced Functional Materials, vol. 25, pp. 2537-2542, 2015, doi: 10.1002/adfm.201500314.

Autonomous Electrochemical Sensing Systems for Environmental and Bio Applications

Vladimir. I. Ogurtsov*, Karen Twomey and Miomir Todorovic
Tyndall National Institute, University College Cork, Lee Maltings Complex, Dyke Parade, Cork, Ireland
*e-mail: vladimir.ogurtsov@tyndall.ie

Abstract—**The study describes the development of autonomous portable electrochemical sensing systems for environmental and bio applications by few examples of custom-designed systems. They include a swallowable capsule with wireless communication link for in-vivo gastrointestinal track investigation, an automatic chemical sensing system operating on-board of a robotic fish for detection pollution and monitoring of the water quality in seaport areas and multichannel electrochemical sensing instrumentation with fluidic control of flow-through system for screening the impact of nanomaterial on human health and the environment. The described apparatuses represent complete sensing systems comprising of a portable low-noise anolog front-end under microcontroller regulation which work in pare with a control PC equipped with corresponding signal processing software for handling the signal from a silicon microfabricated chip-based electrochemical sensors tailored to application specification and requirements. Key principles of the system design are considered and the systems operation and performance are discussed.**

Keywords-Electrochemical sensing system; electrochemical cell; microelectrode array; potentiostat; transimpedance amplifier; signal processing software.

I. INTRODUCTION

Nowadays, the necessity of monitoring and detecting different chemical and biochemical components (chemical anylytes, contaminants, toxicants, biomarkers, etc.) in environmental and bio application areas, such as food industry, clinical diagnostics, environmental protection, drug development and security has significantly increased [1]. Commonly, besides the classical for analytical sensing systems requirement on reliable and specific detection of extremely small quantities of chemical and biochemical targets an additional request on real-time autonomous operation at the point of needs moves to the forefront. This demand is often accompanied by the requirement that the sensing systems should be portable (have low weight and size, small power consumption) and be equipped with in-built signal processing and data interpretation algorithms to allow using the analytical system outside of specialised laboratories in an automatic mode with no-live operator. The role of the intelligent chemical sensing system capable of analyte quantification without user intervention is of great importance for emerging Internet of Things (IoT) devices, where they form an essential part of the IoT environment [2].

The most of traditional analytical methods, which are used to detect the chemical targets, are slow, expensive and require bulky and power hungry equipment demanding dedicated laboratories and highly skilled personnel to operate with it. In this regards, electrochemical sensing systems are of particular interest for in-situ autonomous applications as they can be implemented with relatively simple, portable and non-expensive apparatus that can provide for rapid and sensitive measurements in automatic mode. They can detect solid, liquid or gaseous analytes in different mediums including complex bio fluids with simple operating procedures without or with limited sample pre-treatment that is the essential condition for their implementation outside of the laboratory environment. Emerging microfabrication technologies allowing for manufacturing of micro and nano size electrodes and sensors are boosted an additional interest to electrochemical analytical systems.

Miniaturised electrochemical sensors offer a number of advantages over macroscopic devices including increased mass transport and hence improved sensitivity (due to the hemispherical diffusion), reduced *iR* drop and enhanced signal to noise ratio [3]. Thus, microfabricated electrochemical sensors can achieve the required limits of detection that could not be reached for portable in-field applications before. Additionally, in regards to bioanalytical applications, the micro- and nanobiosensors become comparable in dimensions to many of the biological entities (cells, enzymes, antibodies) appeared to be the detection targets that provides the potential to resolve many of currently unsolved challenges in biosensing.

The described circumstances explain the considerable recent attention that has focused on the development of analytical systems based on a range of electrochemical sensors and microsystems. These devices span diverse applications, including clinical diagnostics [4][5], monitoring of environmental pollutants [6][7], control of food safety [8], detection of bioterrorism agents [9], etc.

On instrumentation part there are a number of various commercial electrochemical equipment available on the market that can be used for lab based applications. At the same time, in many cases end-user and application requirements related to operability in field conditions, ease of use and maintenance, high reliability, fast analysis time, portability (small size, weight and power) and intelligence are so specific that cannot be met with available commercial hardware therefore necessitate custom development of the sensing system to comply with the application specification. In order to match these requirements, very often the full scale development of the sensing system should be undertaken including design of the electrochemical sensor, instrumentation hardware and software [9]-[15]. In the current study, the most attention will be given to instrumentation aspects of the electrochemical sensing systems. Although in recent time system-on-a-chip technologies are increasingly used in the design of the electrochemical instrumentation [12][16] the utilizing of-the-shelf component in the development is still relevant especially when a device series is not expected to be high and device cost is required to be low. Few examples of such custom hardware development are reported below.

The main problems of the instrumentation analog front-end design are discussed in section 2. Then the electrochemical sensing system development illustrated by custom-designed devices, such as a swallowable capsule with wireless communication link for in-vivo gastrointestinal track investigation, an automatic chemical sensing system operating on-board of a robotic fish for detection pollution and monitoring of the water quality in seaport areas and multichannel electrochemical sensing instrumentation with fluidic control of flow-through system for screening the impact of nanomaterial on human health and the environment.

II. Electrochemical instrumentation

In general, an electrochemical sensing system comprises an electrochemical cell incorporating a sensor or sensor array and a mix signal instrumentation hardware. The latter consists of analog front-end, which includes two main electronic units, a potentiostat and a Trans Impedance Amplifier (TIA), and a microcontroller. The analog front-end connects to the microcontroller that controls the measurements and provides data acquisition and connectivity to a control computer. Depending on application requirements the control computer can be a laptop/desktop computer (PC) or a single board computer (i.e., Gumstix, Raspberry Pi, Aurdino, etc.). The electrochemical cell is usually a three electrode structure comprising a Counter Electrode (CE), a Reference Electrode (RE) and a Working Electrode/electrodes (WE) operating as a sensor, which is immersed into or covered by a sample solution to be analyzed. The potentiostat is responsible for setting a stimulation potential between the working and reference electrodes to initiate a redox reaction associated with electron transfer processes between the WE and the solution under investigation. The RE is used as a point of reference in the electrochemical cell; the CE is in charge of closing the current loop with the WE; and WE is the electrode on which surface the electrochemical reaction is happen. This reaction is accompanied with the current related to the target concentration. The current is measured by a TIA and after corresponding signal processing is used for extracting information on target concentration.

However, the signal processing is complicated by a non-faradaic current component attributed to charging of an electrical double layer capacitance and adsorption/desorption processes taking place at the interface of WE and surrounding solution. The double layer capacitance depends on a number of factors including electrode potential, temperature, ionic concentrations, types of ions, oxide layers, electrode roughness, impurity adsorption, etc. Its specific value falls within the range between 20 μF and 60 μF per cm^2 of electrode. Thus, the double-layer capacitance of a 1mm radius disk electrode can be between 0.6 μF and 1.9 μF. This is a significant value that has noticeable effect on performance of the analog front-end and extracting the Faradaic current which is a signal of interest for a great deal of applications.

On signal processing part a number of different electrochemical techniques were suggested to decrease masking effect of the charging current. These techniques use different shapes of the stimulation signal (e.g., DC for amperometry, staircase, square wave, etc. for voltammetry) and perform the current measurement (for voltammetric techniques) at the times when the charging current is significantly decayed after abrupt changes in the stimulation signal. On instrumentation part occurrence of the significant electrode capacitances connected to the analog front-end inputs lead to limitations in the circuit performance and can result in the circuit instability. Therefore, the circuit design should be performed with taking this circumstance into account.

A simplified schematic of the analog part of the electrochemical sensing system is shown in Figure 1

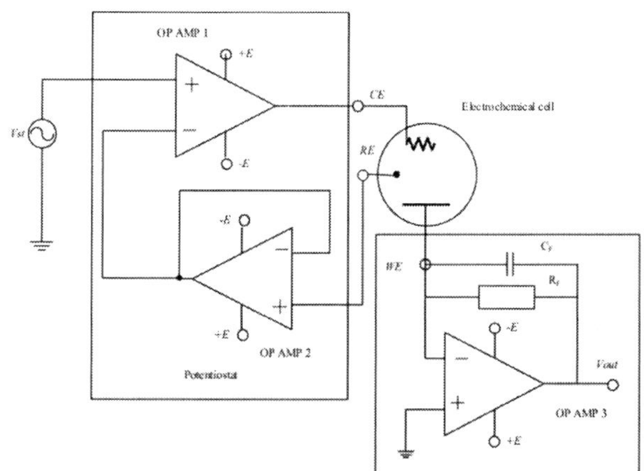

Figure 1. Simplified schematic of the potentiostatic sensing system

The potentiostat is composed of Operational Amplifiers 1 (OP AMP1) and 2 (OP AMP2). The OP AMP1 is the main amplifier that supplies current into the cell; the OP AMP2 serves as a voltage repeater that has high input impedance to eliminate a current flow through the RE. The feedback of the potentiostat is formed by a voltage divider made by the impedance *Zc* (between the CE and the RE) and impedance

Zw (between RE and WE) followed by the voltage repeater. If there is no Faradaic reaction on the electrodes, an equivalent circuit of impedances *Zc* and *Zw* can be represented by serial connection of the corresponding double layer capacitances associated with the corresponding electrodes and liquid resistance between counter or working and reference electrodes. The liquid resistance depends on solution, type of analyte and its concentration, temperature, and the geometry of the electrode system (shape, area and the distance between electrodes). It increases if the distance increases and the electrode area decreases. The potentiostat transfer functions of the stimulation signal to the counter and the reference electrodes are described by eq. (1) and eq. (2) where G_1 and G_2 are frequency dependent open gains of the corresponding OP AMPs, and *Zo* is output resistance of OP AMP1.

$$G_{CE} = \left(1+\frac{Zc}{Zw}\right) \Big/ \left[\frac{1}{1+1/G_2} + \frac{1}{G_1}\left(1+\frac{Zc+Zo}{Zw}\right)\right] \quad (1)$$

$$G_{RE} = 1 \Big/ \left[\frac{1}{1+1/G_2} + \frac{1}{G_1}\left(1+\frac{Zc+Zo}{Zw}\right)\right] \quad (2)$$

Due to serial connection of the two operational amplifier the phase margin can reduce and cause ringing and even instability of the potentiostatic circuit. To avoid it, the repeater amplifier should have the bandwidth significantly larger than the main amplifier. If the circuit stability is secured and DC gains for OP AMPs are significant ($|G2|>>1$ and $|G1|>>|1+(Zc+Zo)/Zw|$, the signal at reference electrode will follow stimulation signal with a small shift that is the smaller, the larger G2 and G1. In this case, the signal at the counter electrode will be defined by 1+Zc/Zw and therefore it can exceed the stimulation signal (if $|Zc/Zw|>>1$). Thus the electrochemical cell should be designed in such a manner that to avoid it.

The presence of the large capacitance in the impedance of the WE connected to the input of the transimpedance amplifier is also can cause instability and ringing of the circuit. The standard approach to optimize the TIA performance is to add a bypass capacitor C_F in parallel with the TIA feedback resistance R_F in order to compensate phase shift and to guarantee sufficient phase margin for stable operation of TIA [17]. However, overcompensation reduces the usable bandwidth of the amplifier thus in case of application requirement on frequency bandwidth the selection of the C_F should be made very carefully.

III. EXAMPLES OF THE ELECTROCHEMICAL SENSING SYSTEM

Electrochemical sensing system with wireless communication link implemented in a swallowable capsule format [15] was developed for in-vivo investigation of gastrointestinal track (GI). The capsule approach, which is as an alternative to the classical invasive methods of GI tract analysis such as endoscopy and colonoscopy, is receiving more research attention in recent years [18]. The suggested solution differs from other capsule based technologies and proposes for examination of GI status to use an electrochemical signature of different GI tract areas instead of taking their images. The solution is represented a complete electrochemical sensing system comprising of electrode system on chip, analog front-end discussed above, microcontroller, wireless transmitter with antenna, and power unit with a single lithium-ion cell battery. These functional units integrated were assembled on a polyimide flexible substrate which was arranged in a fold manner and encapsulated in polyether ether ketone (PEEK) material to fit a capsule with dimensions 12 mm in diameter and 28 mm in length (volume is 3.2 cm3, weight is 7.4 g) (Figure 2). The sensing electrode structure was realized as a 6 x 6 mm2 square silicon die. The largest electrode is a counter electrode. It is a 2 mm diameter disk made of platinum. Four smaller electrodes are 1 mm disks made of gold. Three of these small electrodes connected together were played role of the working electrodes; the fourth disk was plated with platinum and was used as a pseudo reference electrode. The analog front-end of the system was realized with low power, precision JFET AD8643 amplifiers; the microcontroller was PIC18F microcontroller that was chosen for design due to its small package size (6×6 mm^2) and low power consumption; wireless communication link was performed with the help of TH72015, which is a Melexis communication solution implemented in a 3×3 mm^2 QFN package. It has integrated PLL and operates with frequency shift key modulation in the 433 MHz ISM band. The developed capsule was capable of performing cyclic, differential pulse voltammetries in autonomous mode.

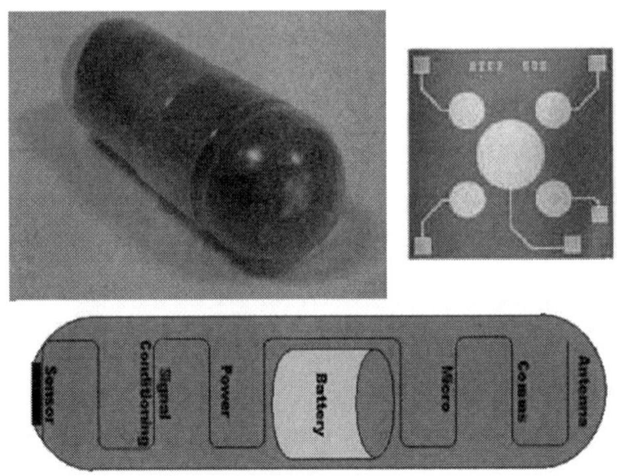

Figure 2. Electrochemical sensing system with wireless communication implemented in capsule format

Laboratory evaluation of the capsule performance confirmed that it could operate over 72 h (estimation of the maximum time of capsule passage through GI tract) and provide at least 500 measurement cycles followed by corresponding wireless data transmission from inside of body at a distance of 1.5 m from the patient.

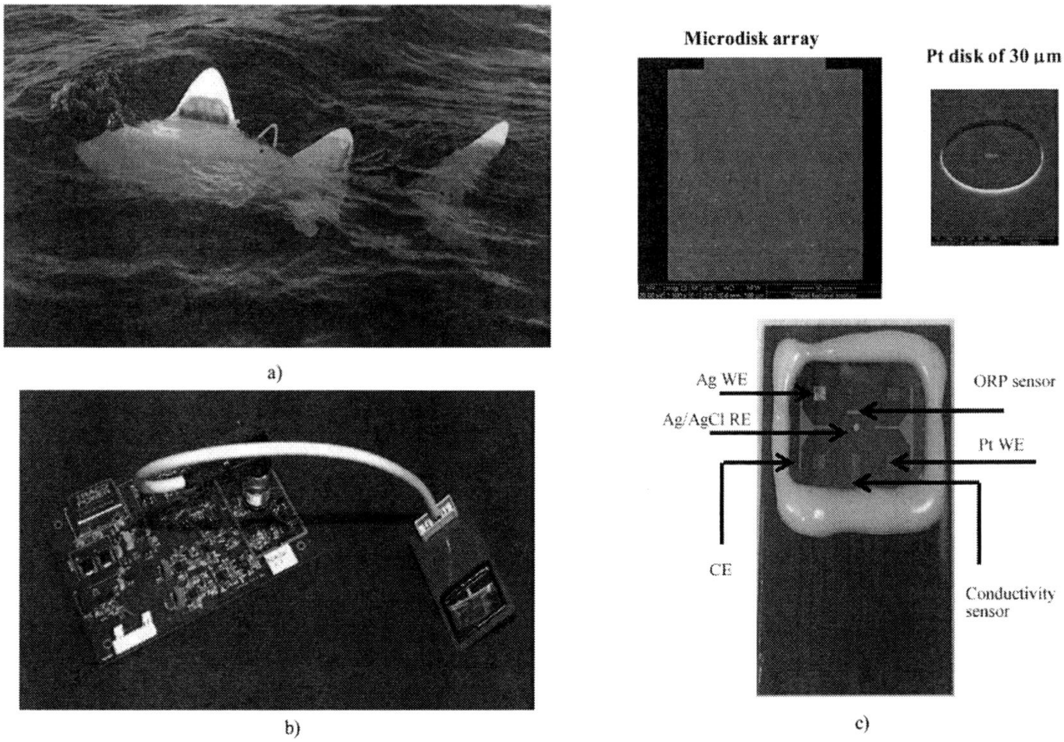

Figure 3. Robotic fish (a) with smart electrochemical sensing instrumentation hardware (b) and packaged sensor chip (c)

The smart chemical sensing system (Figure 3) capable of autonomous operation on-board of a robotic fish for monitoring and detection pollution in water area of seaports was developed to provide real time in-situ detection and measurement of contaminants including heavy metals (ions of Cu2+) and phenol derivatives and sea water quality parameters: dissolved oxygen, oxidation-reduction potential (ORP) and sea water conductivity [14]. The sensing system consisted of four channel potentiostatic system for quantification of chemical analytes, impedimetric circuitry for evaluation of sea water conductivity and low noise high impedance voltage repeater for measurement of ORP. Multiparametric sensing device was implemented onto a single micro fabricated silicon chip with 20×30 mm^2 dimensions. The chip contained two platinum counter electrodes electrically-connected in parallel, three rectangular Pt microdisc arrays and a rectangular Ag microdisc array, which played a part of the working sensing electrodes, a circular silver-based reference electrode, which was common for all working electrodes, a Pt interdigitated electrodes for impedimetric measurement and an ORP electrode. For improving sensor sensitivity the working electrodes were realized as a microdics array. Sixty four discs of 30 μm diameter and separated each other by 300 μm were arranged in a hexagonal structure [14]. The impedimetric sensor for conductivity measurements was made of two interdigitated electrodes. Number of electrode pairs was 40, the electrode width and length was 20 μm and 1500 μm correspondingly, inter electrode distance was 40 μm. Selection platinum rather than gold as material for working electrodes was related to the better stability of Pt to the impact from seawater. The control computer was Gumstix. The system was of 152×52×26 mm^3 dimensions and provided for the autonomous measurements of all parameters in real time with pollution detection limit of 0.2 μM for cupper and 11.2 μM for phenol.

Comprehensive multichannel scalable instrumentation for toxicity assessment is a main part of the smart non-animal high throughput platform for screening the impact of nanomaterials on human and environment. The sensors are based on biological objects including DNA, miRNA, membrane lipids, single cells and lung, intestine, liver, kidney and placenta cells. Each channel includes a wafer-based sensor located inside of a flow chamber of the microfluidic module shown in Figure 4.

Fluidic hardware of the module comprises of 13 solenoid pinch valves, peristaltic and vacuum pumps providing capability of implementation different fluidic protocols including: System filling, Cells cultivation, Exchange („harvesting“). The design of the fluidic system allows for combination of fluidic modules in a complex system to simulate bio interaction between different organs. Instrumentation provides full automated multichannel fluidic flow control synchronized with electrochemical examination of the cell-based sensors. The channel hardware consists of Microfluidic Control Unit (MCU) and Electrochemical Sensing Unit (ESU) each of 60 x 105 x 165 mm^3 dimensions. MCU and ESU units are equipped with corresponding user-friendly software (Figure 5) with in-built signal processing to automate toxicity assessment and simplify its protocol development.

Figure 4. Microfluidic module with fluidic hardware.

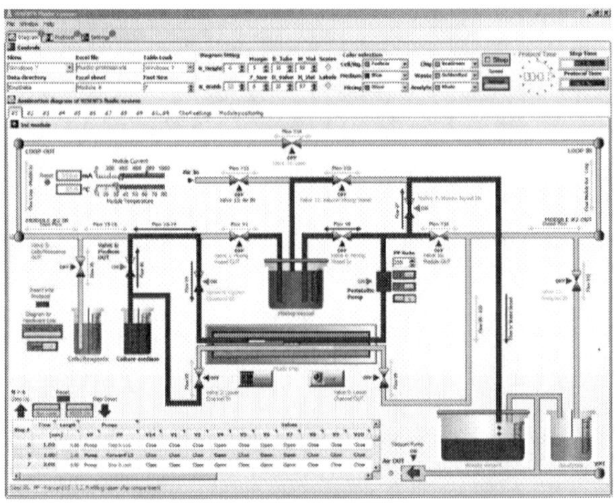

Figure 5. User-friendly software by an example of fluidic diagram tab of MCU module

The number of channels corresponds to the number of the microfluidic modules; channel measurements are synchronised with operation of corresponding microfluidic flow module. Extension of the channels is performed by cable connection of the modules to the common SPI bus.The key features of electronic instrumentation are easy channel extensions, independent or synchronised work MCU with the sensing instrumentation, intelligence, possibility to work under main PC operational systems and in different environments (i.e., NET, LabVIEW, MATLAB). The microfluidic control unit besides of providing full pumping and valve switching control is allowed for decreasing power consumption, smart control of the fluidic hardware command fulfilment, overheating, overcurrent and short circuit protections, module current and temperature monitoring.

Electrochemical sensing unit is realized as a multichannel mix signal scalable system. It is implemented with the following key off-the-shelf electronic components: microcontroller Atxmega128A1U and 16 bit DAC LTC2641 (the digital part), ADA4807 and AD8622 (potentiostat) and ADA4350 and AD8253 (TIA) OP AMPs for the analog front-end of the channel hardware. The potentiostat is capable of provided stimulus signal with scan rate up to 100V/s in the in -3V – +3V range; transimpedance amplifier secured the frequency bandwidth of 41.28 kHz with WE capacitance CS = 10nF with RF = 1M and CF = 4pF (expected bandwidth calculated according recommendation [17] was 40 kHz). Each ESU channel/module acts as a low noise, analog front-end highly sensitive measurement unit under microcontroller control capable of simultaneous and independent from other channels operation. The ESU module provides voltammetric or impedance measurements in three or two electrode configurations correspondingly. Example of voltammetric measurements obtained with the developed ESU for a three electrode electrochemical cell (CE - Pt wire, RE - Silver/Silver chloride, WE - 40 um microdisk gold electrode array) in solution of 0.1M Ferrocyanide in 0.1M KCl at scan rate of 100 mV/s is shown in Figure 6.

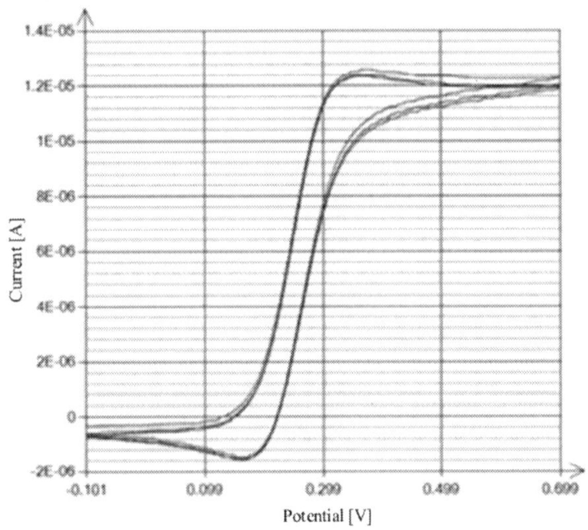

Figure 6. Voltammogram obtained by developed electrochemical sensing module with 40 um gold disk array in 0.1M Ferrocyanide in 0.1M KCl at scan rate of 100 mV/s.

As one can see the voltammogramm has a sigmoidal shape as expected in case of microdisc electrodes. Comparison of the results obtained with the developed sensing system and with a commercial electrochemical station CH 620a showed their good agreement.

IV. Conclusion

Nowadays, electrochemical sensing systems are rapidly transforming from the research laboratory based bulky equipment in autonomous portable systems capable of working at point of needs in an automatic mode with no-live operator. Such platforms are key of importance for environmental and bio applications as they often require real time continuous monitoring and detection different targets in complex media in field conditions. The combination of emerging silicon based sensing microfabricated platforms, state of art electronic instrumentation, microcontroller and signal processing technologies promise to address main challenges of such systems such as sensitivity, portability and intelligence to enable the whole systems to provide required multiparametric real time sensing. The presented in the study examples of custom-designed systems including a swallowable capsule with wireless communication link for in-vivo gastrointestinal track investigation, an automatic chemical sensing system operating on-board of a robotic fish for detection pollution and monitoring of the water quality in seaport areas and multichannel electrochemical sensing instrumentation with fluidic control of flow-through system for screening the impact of nanomaterial on human health and the environment demonstrate possible directions for implementing of these system in practical environmental and bio applications.

ACKNOWLEDGMENT

Financial support of this work by European Commission National Development Plan and Enterprise Ireland (project CFTD05/112 DIACAPS (DIAgnostic CAPSule), European Commission (projects FP7-ICT-231646 "SHOAL: Search and monitoring of harmful contaminants, other pollutants and leaks in vessels in port using a swarm of robotic fishes" and H2020-NMP-29-2015 "HISENTS: High level Integrated SEnsor for NanoToxicity Screening") is gratefully acknowledged.

REFERENCES

[1] J. Fraden. Handbook of Modern Sensors. Physics, Designs, and Applications. , Springer, 2016.

[2] Smart Sensors at the IoT Frontier, Editors H.Yasuura, Ch-M. Kyung, Y. Liu, and Y-L. Lin, Springer, 2018.

[3] D. W. M. Arrigan, "Nanoelectrodes, Nanoelectrode Arrays and Their Applications", Analyst, vol. 129, pp. 1157–1165, 2004

[4] T. Bryan, X. Luo, P. R. Bueno, and J. J. Davis, "An optimised electrochemical biosensor for the label-free detection of C-reactive protein in blood", Biosensors and Bioelectronics, vol. 39(1), pp. 94–98, 2013

[5] J. V. Rushworth, A. Ahmed, H. H. Griffiths, N. M. Pollock, N. M. Hooper, and P. A. Millner "A label-free electrical impedimetric biosensor for the specific detection of Alzheimer's amyloid-beta oligomers", Biosensors and Bioelectronics, vol. 56, pp. 83–90, 2014

[6] X. Wang, X. Lu, and J. Chen "Development of biosensor technologies for analysis of environmental contaminants", Trends in Environmental Analytical Chemistry, vol. 2, pp. 25–32, 2014

[7] W. Moujahid, P. Eichelmann-Daly, J. Strutwolf, V. I. Ogurtsov, G. Herzog, and D. W. M. Arrigan, "Microelectrochemical Systems on Silicon Chips for the Detection of Pollutants in Seawater", Electroanalysis, vol. 23 (1), pp. 147 – 155, 2011

[8] R. Ramesh, P. Puhazhendi, J. Kumar, M. K. Gowthaman, S. F. D'Souza, and N. R. Kamini, "Potentiometric biosensor for determination of urea in milk using immobilized Arthrobacter creatinolyticus urease", Materials Science and Engineering: C, vol. 49(0), pp. 786-792, 2015

[9] V. I. Ogurtsov, K. Twomey, and J. Pulka, "A Portable Sensing System for Impedance based Detection of Biotoxin Substances", Proceedings of the 10th International Joint Conference on Biomedical Engineering Systems and Technologies, vol1: BIODEVICES, pp. 54-62, 2017, Porto, Portugal

[10] V. Beni, V. I. Ogurtsov, N. V. Bakounine, D. W. M Arrigan and M. Hill, "Development of a portable electroanalytical system for the stripping voltammetry of metals: determination of copper in acetic acid soil extracts", Anal. Chim. Acta, vol 552 (1-2), pp. 190-200, 2005.

[11] V. I. Ogurtsov et al., "Miniaturized Electrochemical Sensing System for in Vitro and in Vivo Biomedical Applications", Proceedings of the International Conference on Biomedical Electronics and Devices, pp. 83 – 87, Porto, Jan 14-17 2009.

[12] C. Mc Caffrey, J. Doyle, V. I. Ogurtsov, K. Twomey, and D. W. M. Arrigan, "Development and evaluation of an on-chip potentiostat for biomedical applications", Procedings of the 3rd International Conference on Biomedical Electronics and Devices, BIODEVICE, pp. 103-107, Valencia. Spain, 2010

[13] V. I. Ogurtsov, K. Twomey, and G. Herzog, "Development of an Electrochemical Sensing System for Environmental Monitoring of Port Water Quality to Integrate On-board an Autonomous Robotic Fish", Chapter in Comprehensive Materials Processing Technology, vol. 13, Sensor Materials and Technologies, Elsevier Science, pp. 317–351, 2014

[14] G. Herzog, W. Moujahid, K. Twomey, C. Lyons, and V. I. Ogurtsov, "On-chip electrochemical microsystems for measurements of copper and conductivity in artificial seawater", Talanta, vol. 116, pp. 26–32, 2013.

[15] C. Mc Caffrey, K. Twomey, and V. I. Ogurtsov. "Development of a Wireless Swallowable Capsule with Potentiostatic Electrochemical Sensor for Gastrointestinal Track Investigation", Sensors & Actuators: B. Chemical, vol. 218, pp. 8-15, 2015.

[16] Y-T. Liu, M. Chen, Z-C. Li, Y. Wang, and J. Chen, "A high dynamic range analog-front-end IC for electrochemical amperometric and voltammetric sensors", Microelectronics Journal, vol. 46(8), pp. 716-722, 2015

[17] J. G. Graeme, "Photodiode Amplifiers: OP AMP Solutions", McGraw-Hill, Inc. New York, NY, USA, 1996

[18] M. Naoki, T. Kumiko, T. Satoshi, and T. Tetsuji. "Colon capsule endoscopy: toward the future", Clinical Journal of Gastroenterology, vol. 10 (1), pp. 1-6, 2017.

Towards Real Time Imaging and Tracking of Human Organs for Surgical Navigation by Using Artifical Magnetic Fields and MEMS Magnetic Sensor Nodes

Jian Lu*, Dapeng Zhang, Lan Zhang, Ryutaro Maeda
Research Center for Ubiquitous MEMS and Micro Engineering (UMEMSME)
National Institute of Advanced Industrial Science and Technology (AIST)
Namiki 1-2-1, Tsukuba, 305-8564, Japan
*Corresponding author. e-mail: jian-lu@aist.go.jp

Yoichi Okuda, Masanao Kurata, Nobuhiro Ohkohchi
Department of Gastrointestinal and Hepato-Biliary-Pancreatic Surgery, faculty of Medicine
University of Tsukuba
Tennoudai 1-1-1, Tsukuba, 305-8577, Japan

Abstract— **Towards real time imaging of human organs during medical surgeries for organ excision or tumor care, we have been engaged in developing a high-resolution tracking system by using artificial magnetic fields and 3D MEMS magnetic sensor nodes for years. This paper presents fundamentals of this approach, design and simulation of the electromagnetic system for the pursuit of unique magnetic fields with preferable spatial resolution, and configuration of the developed prototypes. The preliminary results reveal that spatial resolution of a few mm can be achieved after applying multi-pairs electromagnetics, which is powered by DC and AC signal respectively for noise cancellation as well as for rotation recognition. Moreover, temperature dependence, background noise of a surgical room, and many other specifications of the developed system were investigated, evaluated, and discussed herein.**

Keywords- surgical navigation; human organ; location tracking; magnetic field; MEMS sensor; MedTech innovation.

I. INTRODUCTION

Advances in electronic devices, robotics, and diagnostic techniques enable widely use of laparoscopic surgery for various diseases [1]-[3]. Laparoscopic surgery is less invasive to patients so quick recovery can be expected, but fatal bleeding may happen due to misunderstanding of vessels and its anatomical location by patient's posture change, etc., especially in the hepateetomy and pancreaticoduodenectomy [4]. Then, mental pressure will be introduced to surgeon during the operation since it is hard to find remedial measures in a very short time with limited capabilities of actions under endoscope. Developing a real time location tracking system for surgical navigation is thus essentially important, especially for liver excisions, which is believed one of the most complicated tasks, i.e., it was reported that third party mortality and 90-day in-hospital mortality rates were as high as 2.0% and 4.0% respectively even in Japan [5].

Trakstar® (Ascension Technology Corp.) [6] and AURORA® (Northern Digital Inc.) [7] are popular systems used for real time electromagnetic tracking of operative devices with imaged-guided simulation applications. Although there is no convincing evidence to suggest that exposure to high-frequency electromagnetic fields will cause any significant adverse health effect in humans [8], the system may introduce interferences to other medical instruments to a certain extend. In addition, due to big size and high cost of micro coils, which is used as the sensor to detect high frequency electromagnetic fields, practical application of above systems for human organs is somehow difficult. High sampling rate is required to achieve sub-mm spatial resolution, so wireless communication between sensors and the system is hard to be realized when number of the sensors increases intentionally.

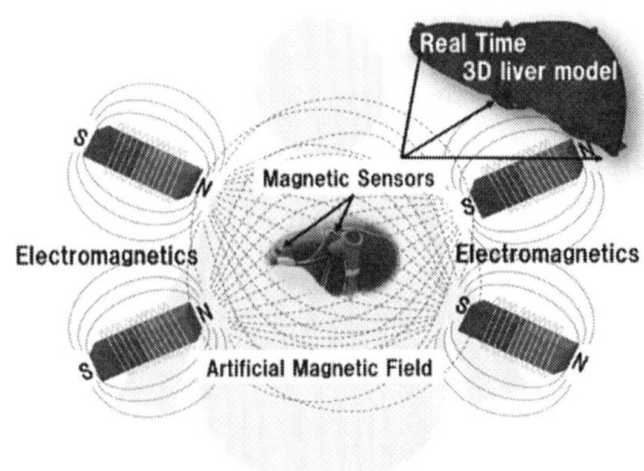

Figure 1. Principe of our proposed location tracking system by using multi-pairs electromagnetics and 3D MEMS magnetic sensors.

Figure 1 shows the principle of the proposed location tracking system. A 3D liver model is established prior to surgery by Computed Tomography (CT) and simulation tools. It is believed that human tissues, organs, etc., will have no effects to static magnetic field, therefore a few pairs electromagnetic are located around human body to create static and ultra-low frequency magnetic fields, in which intensity or direction is unique at individual locations. 3D MEMS magnetic sensors (AK09970, Asahi Kasei Corp.) are attached to specific points of the liver to track location by measuring corresponding intensity and direction of the fields. Tracking results from those sensors are used to update liver model image in real time during surgeries.

In this paper, besides fundamentals of this approach, design and simulation of the electromagnetic field, configuration and specifications of the developed wireless sensor nodes and the location tracking system, as well as preliminary evaluation results are presented in details, and then discussed.

In section 2 of this paper, system configurations will be presented. Experimental details and the results will be presented in section 3 together with discussions. And then, sections 4 will concludes this paper with future plans.

II. System Design and Configurations

To design preferred artificial magnetic fields for the pursuit of a few mm spatial resolution, an magnetic simulator was used to calculate its intensity and direction within the volume of $60\times60\times40$ cm^3. Figure 2 shows calculated results and measured results for comparisons. Distance of the two electromagnetics in each pair was set at 60 cm, and a magnetic path was included in between them to increase intensity at the center of the field. A DC power source was used to supply voltage up to 80 V, which insures that minimum vector intensity is no less than 3 mT, 2 orders bigger than that of earth magnetics.

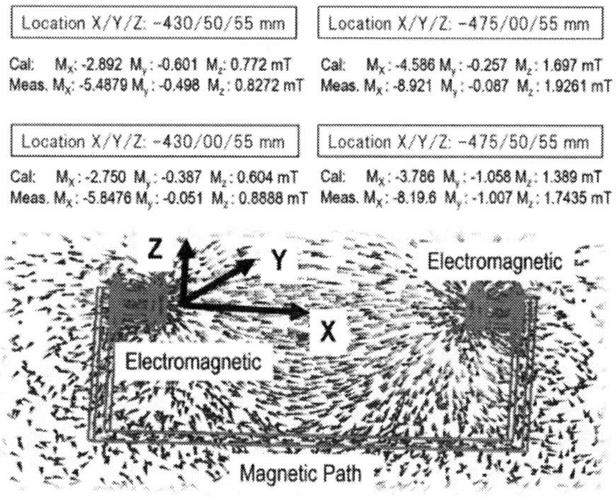

Figure 2. Simulated distribution of the magnetic field in one pair electromagnetics. The measured results are listed too for comparisons.

Figure 2 clearly reveals that the calculated distribution of the field fit well with the measured results, even though the individual data is slightly different due to the difference between model and actual profile of electromagnetics. It also indicates that experimental mapping of the field is essential to create database (also called 'map' in this work) for accurate location tracking. The measured resolution of the field was 76 uT/mm and 18 uT/mm in X and Y direction, respectively. It suggests that sensitivity (1.1uT/LSB) of selected 3D MEMS magnetic sensor is good enough to identify a few mm for surgical navigation as expected in this work.

Since intensity of the field dramatically decreases when its distance to electromagnetic increases, i.e., 3 mT at the center of the field while >30 mT at the surface of the electromagnetics, multi-pairs of electromagnetics were introduced in this system to compensate location variations, as well as to identify rotation of the sensor nodes. Figure 3 shows the photo of the developed 1st prototype system for further investigation and evaluation. To create the 'map' for navigation, a 3D robot with wooden arms were used to carry MEMS magnetic sensors for scanning, while a 3D camera system was used to record the actual location of the sensor simultaneously. Three pairs of electromagnetics were included in the system, among them, one pair was set up under the wooden desk for a more uniform distribution at the center of the field.

ON/OFF switching of all three pairs of electromagnetics in turn may help to separate the magnetic field created by each pair. However, as shown in Figure 4, it will lead to difficulties in real time tracking because 2-3 seconds is required to stabilize each magnetic field. Therefore, in this system, the three pairs of electromagnetics were powered simultaneously, among them DC signal was used in the first pair to create static magnetic field, AC signals with

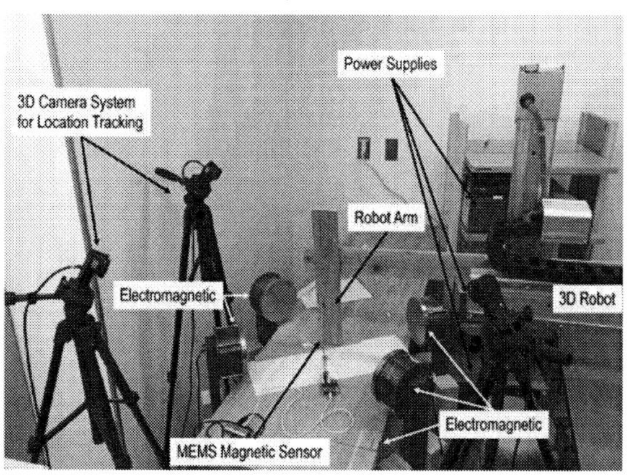

Figure 3. Photo of the develoepd location tracking system with 3D robot system and 3D camera system for further evaluation.

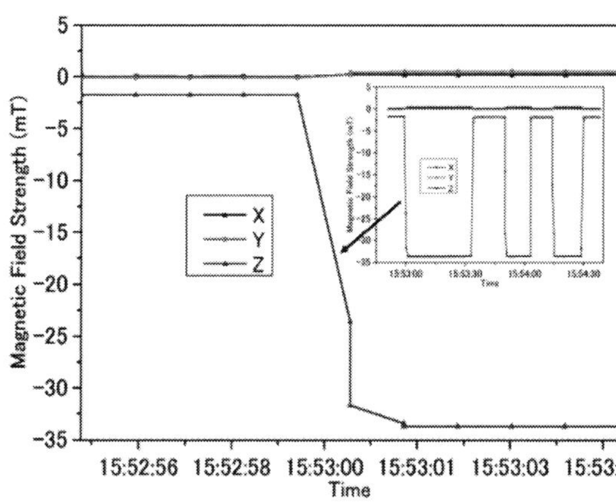

Figure 4. Maesured respponse of the magnetic field when ON/OFF the field by switching power supply.

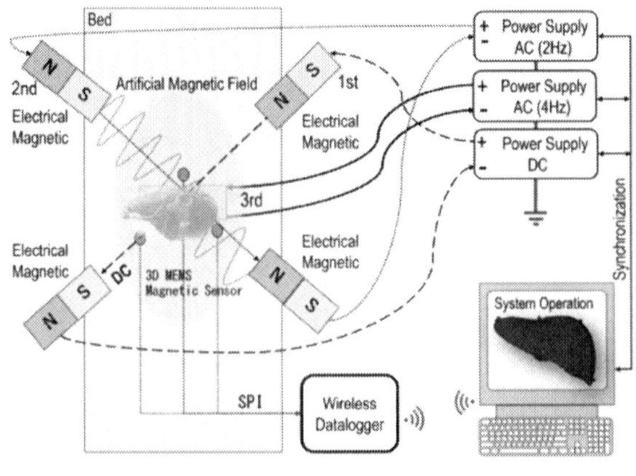

Figure 5. Configurations of the proposed system, which include multi-pairs electromagnetics and its power supply, 3D MEMS magnetic sensors and its signal processing unit, and PC.

frequencies of 1 Hz and 2 Hz were used in the second and the third pair to create ultra-low frequency magnetic field, respectively. Kalman filter [9] and self-developed algorithm were carried out to separate AC and DC signal from the mixed raw data recorded by MEMS magnetic sensors.

Another advantageous of above method is to identify artificial magnetic field from earth magnetic field and background noise by their frequency spectrum. Based on the above considerations and design, layout and configurations of the location tracking system is hen shown in Figure 5.

III. Experimental Results and Discussion

A. Backgound noise

Various types of medical devices and instruments are used in a surgery room to monitor physical signs and biological information of a patient. Figure 6 shows measured electromagnetic noise, especially when turn on electrical knife for organ excision. The measured background noise, 20-30 uT (peak-to-peak value) as shown in Figure 6 (a), is similar or even lower than typical value of earth magnetics, indicating neglectable effects to the positioning system. Although the noise from electrical knife is 2-3 times bigger than background noise, it can be easily removed by using digital filter since its frequency (~0.25Hz) is much lower than that of the developed positioning system. The interferences of the developed positioning system to other medical instruments was not found yet in experiments.

B. Temperature dependence and stabilities

It was found in Figure 7 that temperature was stabilized in 15 min when AC signal was applied. Whereas, temperature of the DC signal powered electromagnetics was keep raising even 55 min after switch the power ON. However, the upper inset of Figure 7 clearly indicated that intensity of the magnetic field was stable without any noticeable dependence on temperatures, thanks to constant current mode of the power supply. Moreover, variation of the DC magnetic field was 300-500 ppm, which is reasonably good for a preferred system resolution.

Above results also suggested that minimum vector intensity of the field can be as small as 1 mT, while keeping system spatial resolution with no remarkable change. It enables us to use much lower power, much smaller electromagnetics, and remove magnetic path to further improve stability of the field. These works are ongoing in the 2nd prototype system.

C. Location tracking accuracy

To achieve a few mm spatial resolution, 1 mm pitch size is required when creating the navigation 'map' as described above. However, it may takes weeks or even months since there are millions of points within the volume of 60×60×

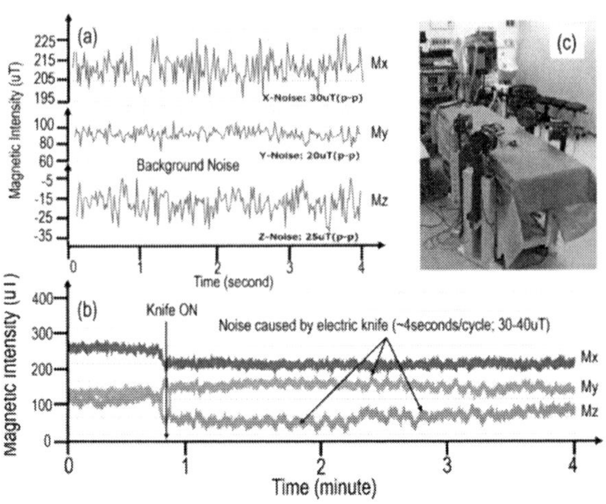

Figure 6. Measured electromagnetic noise in a surgery room (a); electromagnetic noise when using electrical knife a few cm far from the sensor (b); photos of the measurement system (c).

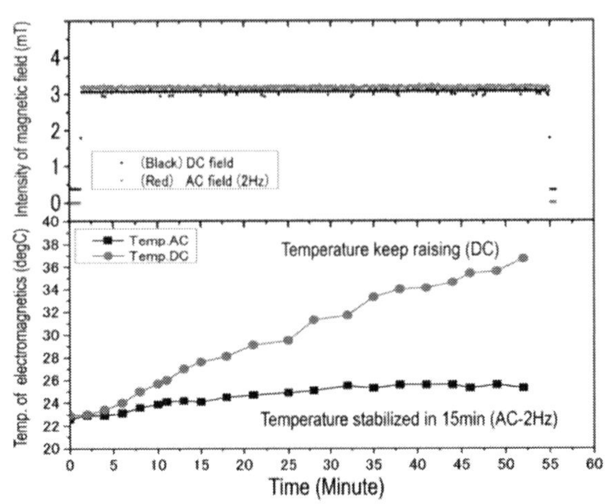

Figure 7. Measured temperature dependance of the electromagnetics and the magnetic field when powered by DC and AC signal, respectively.

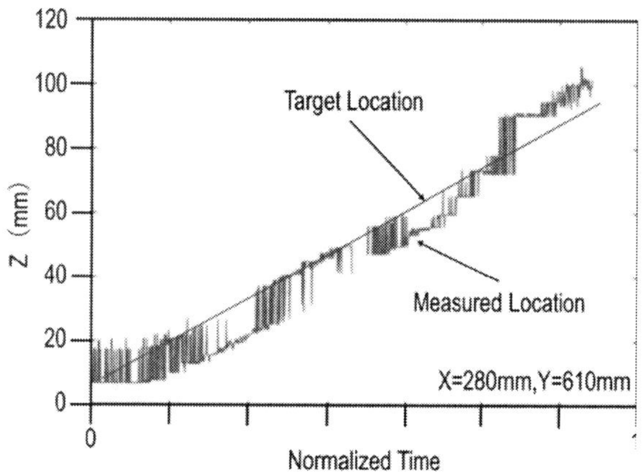

Figure 8. Measured and actual location in Z direction when X and Y was 280mm and 610mm, respectively.

40 cm^3. To demonstrate and evaluate resolution of the system, the pitch was set to 4 mm and created the 'map' within the volume of $8 \times 12 \times 12$ cm^3. As shown in Figure 8, about 11 mm spatial resolution was obtained. This preliminary result is not good enough for a practical application, but sufficient to prove this approach both theoretically and experimentally.

As demonstrated in 2D movement, 2-3 mm spatial resolution was obtained when the pitch size was set at 1 mm during 'map' creation. However, a simulation-based approach for quick database creation is believed necessary to improve efficiency, in which experimental mapping will be required only for system calibration. The lasted results indicated that 1 mm spatial resolution can be obtained, if the pitch size of the database is 1 mm. This work is on progress and the preliminary results are attractive. The details will be presented in future publications.

IV. CONCLUSIONS AND FUTURE WORKS

This paper presents the development and evaluation of a real time imaging and tracking system for surgical navigation by using artificial magnetic fields and MEMS magnetic sensor nodes. Spatial resolution of a few mm was achieved as the preliminary result. It is encouraging and promising at the current stage, while further development and improvement are necessary for practical applications.

As the next step of this work, we will focus on developing the simulation-based approach for creating navigation 'map', as well as system optimization for a better spatial resolution. Animal test is also on the schedule to investigate effectiveness of the system. Moreover, the state-of-the-art research results are not sufficient to draw any conclusions about potential health effects of static magnetic field exposure, while it needs further study to make it clear.

This paper strongly suggested that MedTech innovations, which is extremely important for modern society, can be accelerated by the advances in MEMS and sensing technologies.

ACKNOWLEDGMENT

This work is supported by Japan Agency for Medical Research and Development through "Technological development of a real-time navigation system for laparoscopic hepatectomy with wireless microsensor for tactile sensing and with position monitoring of instrument" project.

REFERENCES

[1] A. Buia, F. Stockhausen, and E. Hanisch, "Laparoscopic Surgery: A Qualigied Systematic Review", World J Methodol, vol. 5, pp. 238-254, Dec. 2015, doi: 10.5662/wjm.v5.i4.238.

[2] H. F. Roh, S. H. Nam, and J. M. Kim, "Robot-assisted Laparoscopic Surgery Versus Conventional Laparoscopic Surgery in Randomized Controlled Trials: A Systematic Review and Meta-analysis", Lops One, Jan. 2018, doi: https://doi.org/10.1371/journal.pone.0191628.

[3] L. Negoi, M. Beuran, et. al "The Lapaoscopic Approach in Emergency Surgery: A Review of the Literature", Journal of Acute Disease, vol. 7, pp. 15-19, April 2018, doi: 10.4103/2221-6189.228873.

[4] R. Miyamoto, Y. Oshiro, K. Nakayama, and N. Ohkohchi. "Impact of Three-dimensional Surgical Simulation on Pancreatic Surgery", Gastrointest. Tumors, vol. 4, pp.84-89, Feb. 2018, doi: 10.1159/000484894.

[5] A. Kenjo, et. al "Risk Stratification of 7,732 Hepatectomy Cases in 2011 from the National Clinical Database for Japan," Journal of the American College of Surgeons, vol. 218, pp. 412-422, Mar. 2014, doi: 10.1016/j.jamcollsurg.2013.11.007.

[6] https://www.ascension-tech.com/

[7] https://www.ndigital.com/

[8] Z. Sienkiewicz, "Biological Effects of Electromagnetic Fields and Radiation", Journal of Radiological Protection, vol. 18, pp. 185-194, doi: https://doi.org/10.1088/0952-4746/18/3/005

[9] D. Loebis, R. Sutton, J. Chudley, and W. Naeem, "Adaptive Tuning of a Kalman Filter via Fuzzy Logic for An Intelligent AUV Navigation System", Control Engineering Practice, vol. 12, pp. 1531-1539, Dec. 2004, doi: https://doi.org/10.1016/j.conengprac.2003.11.008.

Evaluation of Low-Cost/High-Accuracy Indoor Positioning Systems

Robin Amsters,
Eric Demeester
and Peter Slaets
KU Leuven,
Department of Mechanical Engineering,
3000 Leuven, Belgium
Email: {firstname.lastname}@kuleuven.be

Nobby Stevens
KU Leuven,
Department of Electrical Engineering,
3000 Leuven, Belgium
Email:nobby.stevens@kuleuven.be

Quinten Lauwers
KU Leuven,
3000 Leuven, Belgium
Email: quinten.lauwers@student.kuleuven.be

Abstract—**Indoor positioning is a challenging research topic. Over the years, many different measurement principles and algorithms have been proposed. Each system has its own advantages and drawbacks, therefore trade-offs have to be made. For example, one generally needs to make a trade-off between cost and accuracy. However, recent developments in sensing technology have led to commercial systems that advertise sub-decimeter positioning accuracy for less than €1k. In this paper, we benchmark the accuracy of indoor positioning systems by Pozyx labs and Marvelmind robotics, as well as the VIVE tracker by HTC and Aruco Marker tracking in OpenCV. Results show that these systems achieve an average dynamic positioning accuracy of approximately 150 mm, 20 mm, 8 mm and 100 mm, respectively.**

Keywords–Indoor positioning; benchmarking; accuracy

I. Introduction

Positioning is not a particularly new problem. Mankind has attempted to determine his position for centuries, using instruments such as sextants, clocks, almanacs, maps, etc., One of the largest revolutions in this field is probably the advent of the Global Positioning System (GPS), which can provide position information almost anywhere on earth to anyone with a receiver. However, GPS often does not work in indoor environments, as the signals of the satellites lose much strength when penetrating the walls of buildings [1], making it difficult to receive them with traditional, low-cost sensors. Moreover, the accuracy (that is, the Euclidean distance between the true and the reported position) of such sensors is limited to a couple of meters, which is insufficient for many indoor applications. A study performed by the National Exposure Research Laboratory indicates that most people spend about 90% of their time indoors [2]. Therefore, indoor location information provides many business opportunities. This is illustrated by the fact that the indoor mapping market is rapidly increasing in size, and is estimated to be worth about $10 billion by 2020 [3]. As GPS cannot be used for indoor environments, different technologies are required to obtain this position information. While GPS has become the de facto standard for outdoor environments, no such standard exists for indoor spaces [4]. The wide variety of indoor environments has prompted an equally wide variety of Indoor Positioning Systems (IPS), each with their own advantages and drawbacks. Usually, a trade-off has to be made between accuracy and cost. In the past, this trade-off was quite significant. However, in recent years, a number of positioning systems have come to market that should provide high accuracy ($\leq$ 10 cm) at relatively low-cost ($\leq$ € 1k), potentially bridging the gap that existed before. In this paper, we evaluate several commercially available high-accuracy/low-cost indoor positioning systems. Different measurement principles are represented, namely ultrasound, ultrawideband radio, infrared light and computer vision. A highly accurate (sub-millimeter) infrared measurement system is used as a ground truth reference. The positioning systems are benchmarked in the same environment, thus enabling an objective comparison.

The rest of the paper is structured as follows; Section II presents related work and the main contributions of this paper. Section III elaborates on the different positioning systems that were considered. The experimental setup is explained in Section IV, and results are presented in Section V. Finally, a conclusion is drawn in Section VI.

II. Related work

Van Haute et al. [5] benchmarked several indoor positioning systems in a healthcare environment. Low-cost technologies like Wi-Fi, ZigBee and bluetooth low-energy (BLE) were used. Accuracy of static measurements in the order of 1 to 4 meters was obtained. These kinds of radio-frequency (RF) based systems are relatively popular for indoor localization, due to the widespread availability of the hardware. However, accuracy is rarely below 1 meter [1].

Ultrawideband (UWB) has been an increasingly important topic in indoor positioning research in recent years. Typically, UWB positioning systems determine the distance between static anchors and a mobile node based on signal travel time. A position estimate is then obtained via triangulation. Ruiz and Seco [6] compared the commercial UWB systems sold by DecaWave (the Pozyx system uses DecaWave transceivers) and BeSpoon. Manual measurements with a ruler were used as ground truth. Ruiz and Granja [7] added the Ubisense system to this comparison, and extended the testing space to a larger industrial warehouse as well (rather than the lab environment as in [6]). A comparison was made based on the ranging accuracy and positioning accuracy with a particle filter. An overview of the positioning results of these papers can be found in Table I. The Ubisense system was evaluated separately as well by Maleek and Sadeghpour [8]. The focus of their work was dynamic positioning and localization of factory workers in order to increase safety. A number of experiments were performed by placing a tag on a Lego track, as well as experiments where the tag was used to localize a person. Ground truth locations are calculated based on the starting time and the known layout of the lego track for the first set of experiments. For the experiments on worker localization, the real position was determined with a robotics total station (Leica iCON Robot 50). Their findings indicate 2D accuracy of 15-31 cm depending on the experiment. Dabove et al. evaluated the Pozyx system in [9]. In an office environment, the average 3D positioning accuracy was 100 mm, and the accuracy of the range measurements was found to be 320 mm. In a narrow corridor, the horizontal accuracy and range error were determined to be 87.4 mm and 225 mm, respectively. Surveying equipment was used as ground truth reference for static range measurements, and a grid pattern was used for static positioning ground truth measurements. Finally, Ridolfi et al. [10] evaluated the Pozyx kit as a positioning technology for sports postures. Average positioning errors of 200 mm were recorded (depending on tag placement and activity) and the authors propose several implementations of filtering algorithms to reduce this error. A motion capture system (MOCAP) was used as ground truth.

TABLE I. OVERVIEW OF PREVIOUS UWB BENCHMARKING RESULTS REPORTED IN [6] AND [7]. P90 REPRESENTS THE 90% INTERVAL OF THE CUMULATIVE ERROR DISTRIBUTION

	DecaWave	BeSpoon	Ubisense
Mean accuracy (office) [m]	0.24	0.51	/
P90 (office) [m]	0.51	0.99	/
Mean accuracy (factory) [m]	0.49	0.71	1.1
P90 (factory) [m]	1.09	1.16	2.39

The ranging of the Marvelmind system was, to the best of our knowledge, only benchmarked by Cernohorsk and Novk [11]. The error of the range measurements was found to be in the order of a few centimeters, though some outliers exist in absence of a direct line of sight. The absolute positioning error was not evaluated.

The HTC VIVE is a relatively new system, and thus little research about it is available. Chang et al. [12] compared several head-mounted virtual reality systems, namely the 3Glasses D2, Oculus Rift DK2, Google Cardboard and Samsung Gear VR based on metrics such as positioning precision and sensitivity. One degree of freedom motion was considered by mounting the headsets on a servo motor. However, the HTC VIVE was not considered. Niehorster et al. [13] did evaluate the precision and latency of the HTC VIVE specifically. Latency is conservatively estimated to be 22 ms, significantly less than the latency of the 3Glasses D2 (44 ms) and Oculus Rift DK2 (48 ms) measured by Chang et al. [12]. Niehorster et al. concluded that the VIVE measures at a tilted reference plane relative to the ground plane. However, the angles and positions reported by the VIVE are consistent as long as the system does not lose tracking. Positioning accuracy was not reported.

It is clear that while some of these systems have been evaluated in previous publications, further work is still required. For example, position accuracy is not always specified and even when reported, this is often the average value. In the context of, for example, autonomous operation of mobile robots, one is often also interested in the P95, that is, the 95% interval of cumulative error distribution. These results are usually not included ([6] and [7] do report 90% intervals, as shown in Table I). Additionally, static grid measurements or measurements with a ruler are often used as a ground truth reference. A survey of papers published in the proceedings of the International Conference on Indoor Positioning and Indoor Navigation (IPIN) concludes that this method is used quite often in indoor positioning research [14]. In this work, we perform ground truth measurements with a highly (sub-millimeter) accurate positioning system with a relatively high update rate (50 Hz, see Section IV). This allows better characterization of the dynamic performance of the considered indoor positioning systems.

In summary, our main contributions are:

- Evaluation of several measurement principles in the same environment.
- Measurements of moving receivers are compared with a highly accurate, fast-measuring ground truth reference.
- Evaluation of positioning accuracy, rather than ranging distance.
- Reporting of mean accuracy and P95 values, to provide both an overview of normal performance and worst case scenarios.

III. SYSTEMS UNDER EVALUATION

Table II provides an overview of the main specifications of the IPS considered in this paper. The system cost includes value added tax, and the specifications for the Aruco system are based on the camera used in this work (Logitech HD webcam). Scalability refers to whether a particular system can easily be extended up to larger environments.

The indoor positioning system by Marvelmind robotics uses ultrasound ranging to determine the position of one or more mobile sensor modules (referred to as hedgehogs). Ultrasound ranging is also used by the transmitters (referred to as beacons) to determine their relative position. Therefore, the Marvelmind system is self-calibrating. The sensor modules have built-in rechargeable batteries, and whether a module is a beacon or hedgehog can be selected in the software and changed at will. The maximum update rate for tracking a single hedgehog is 16 Hz. The system uses time division multiplexing, so if multiple hedgehogs are tracked, the update rate becomes:

$$F_{update} = \frac{16}{n_{hedgehog}} \quad (1)$$

With F_{update} the update rate of every hedgehog and $n_{hedgehog}$ the number of tracked hedgehogs.

The indoor positioning system by Pozyx labs uses ultrawideband radio as a distance estimation principle. Additionally, data from a 9-axis Inertial Measurement Unit (IMU) is fused in order to improve the position estimate. The advantage of ultrawideband over other RF technologies is that the increased bandwidth makes it more likely that at least some of the transmitted frequencies will go through or around obstacles [15]. Therefore, accuracy can be significantly higher than, for example, Bluetooth or Wi-Fi based positioning [4]. The system has the option to self-calibrate, but we performed a manual calibration to improve accuracy [16] (see Section V-B).

The HTC VIVE is sold as a virtual reality headset, and ships with a Head-Mounted Display (HMD), two controllers with infrared receivers and two infrared transmitters (called lighthouses). Recently, a standalone tracker module has also been released to enable simpler tracking of objects [17]. It is the positioning of the tracker that was evaluated in this paper. Each lighthouse is equipped with two lasers, which sweep across its horizontal and vertical axes. The infrared laser sweeps are detected by photodiodes which are mounted on the controllers, headset or tracker modules. The difference between arrival times of the laser at the photodiodes is used to determine the position and orientation of the modules [13]. These laser measurements function mostly as drift correction. In between sweeps, positions are estimated with IMU-based dead-reckoning [18]. Contrary to the other systems considered in this paper, the VIVE was not originally designed to be a standalone positioning system. However, accurate position and orientation tracking is required to provide a good virtual reality user experience. As the OpenVR Software Development Kit (SDK) has a published driver for the tracking hardware [19], it is possible to access all the tracking information outside a gaming environment, thus opening the door for a wide range of other applications. As a positioning system, however, the user experience is not as smooth as the Pozyx or Marvelmind systems. For example, steamVR needs to be continuously running in the background and the controllers need to be connected even if one only wants to know the position of the tracker. At the time of writing, it is also not possible to utilize more than 2 lighthouses, thus limiting the operating space.

The final positioning system considered in this work is based on Aruco marker detection [20] with a webcam and OpenCV. The field of computer vision has many examples of marker tracking, the implementation in this paper is likely not the most accurate or user friendly system available. For example, a calibration procedure is required to compensate for the effects of lens distortion and to convert the measured coordinates from pixels to meters [21]. The system is nonetheless included in this comparison as a representative example of what a novice in the field could reasonably implement themselves, and represents one of the lowest cost IPS that can achieve sub-decimeter accuracy. The system returns z-coordinates, but these should not be used as it is challenging to estimate depth with a monocular camera.

TABLE II. SPECIFICATIONS OF THE CONSIDERED IPS.

Positioning system	Marvelmind	HTC VIVE	Pozyx	Aruco
Update rate (max) [Hz]	16	120	138	30
Approximate system cost [€]	400	700	600	70
Measurement range [m]	50	5	30	
Scalable ?	Yes	No	Yes	No

IV. EXPERIMENTAL SETUP

Experiments were conducted in a lab environment of approximately 5 meters by 5 meters. All beacons were mounted at the edges of the test space. The Pozyx beacons are mounted vertically at approximately the height of the receiver (see Section V-B). The lighthouses for the VIVE are attached to metal poles and pointed slightly downwards. Both the Marvelmind beacons and the webcam are attached to the ceiling at a height of approximately 2.8 meters. Figure 1 shows the experimental setup. The receivers of the various positioning systems are mounted on top of a mobile robot with a custom sensor platform (see Figure 2). The Pozyx tag is mounted vertically to improve accuracy [16]. The tag is connected to a raspberry pi 3 that also controls the robot. Measurements for the HTC VIVE, Marvelmind and camera system are received on a laptop. The robot moves at varying speeds during the experiments, occasionally stopping to turn. The maximum speed of the platform is about 0.2 m/s.

As a ground truth reference, the Krypton K600 coordinate measurement machine (CMM) was used. This system is equipped with 3 infrared cameras, which track the positions of infrared LEDs that can be attached to objects. The accuracy of the system is between 60 μm and 190 μm, depending on the distance to the camera [22]. The krypton CMM is controlled with and measurements are stored on a separate computer.

Figure 1. Experimental setup. One more Pozyx beacon is present but cannot be seen on this perspective.

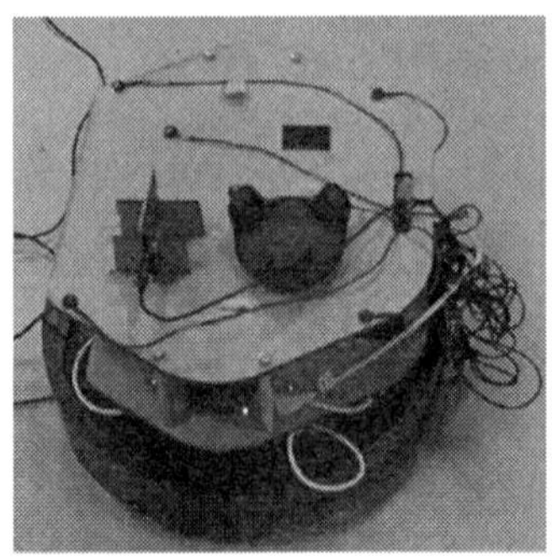

Figure 2. Robot platform used in the experiments

A. Data processing

Data from the systems under testing (SUT) are returned in different formats (e.g., a .txt file for the HTC VIVE and as a rosbag for the Marvelmind system). In order to compare data from different systems, all the output is first converted to a CSV file containing the timestamped positions. It is assumed that timestamps recorded by different computers only have an offset difference.

Following conversion, both the CSV data from the Krypton CMM and the SUT are loaded into memory. The positions of the infrared LEDs relative to the robot center are used to determine the robot pose via Procrustes analysis [23] and Kabsch algorithm [24], which determines the least-squares solution for the pose matrix. Next, these pose matrices and the position of the evaluation system relative to the robot center are used to calculate the equivalent trajectory of the SUT (that is, the trajectory that the SUT would report if it was placed at the location of the krypton markers). However, this equivalent trajectory can still be rotated or translated in space, and have an offset time difference relative to the SUT. Additionally, the sampling frequency of the krypton measurement system is not necessarily the same as the SUT. To determine the points that can be compared, virtual timestamps of the Krypton CMM that provide the best match for the SUT are selected, based on the assumption of a constant 50 Hz sampling rate and the starting time of the experiment. Out of these timestamps, those that overlap are selected for evaluation (see Figure 3). At this stage in the post-processing, we have two datasets of equal length (one equivalent dataset for the Krypton CMM and one for the SUT). The position data can still be rotated and translated relative to each other, and the time vectors can have an offset difference. We therefore calculate the transformation matrix that provides the best fit of the position data. The SUT data is then transformed to the Krypton coordinate frame with this matrix. Next, we shift the timestamps of the evaluation samples with a period of the reference system and calculate the transformed dataset. The time shift that provides the smallest error is assumed to be the offset difference between the clock. The result of this process is a reference dataset and an evaluation dataset that is aligned in space and in time, from which the accuracy can now be computed.

One might argue that the method described above provides the smallest possible positioning errors as the data is transformed to provide the best fit. Therefore, the entire length of the datasets are not fitted to each other. Rather, for each experiment approximately half of the data is used for fitting, and the rest is used for evaluation.

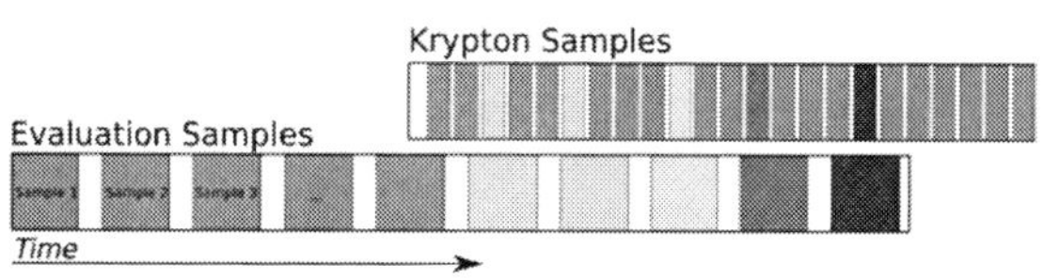

Figure 3. Procedure for determining overlapping samples in the krypton and SUT datasets. Samples in the same color are assumed to represent the same timestep

V. EXPERIMENTAL RESULTS

Table III provides an overview of the measured accuracies of the different positioning systems. The following Sections will elaborate on these results. Accuracy is defined as follows:

$$\varepsilon = \sqrt{(x_{ref} - x_{SUT})^2 + (y_{ref} - y_{SUT})^2 + (z_{ref} - z_{SUT})^2} \quad (2)$$

Where x, y and z are used to denote the different coordinate axes, and the subscripts ref and SUT indicate the ground truth and the system under testing, respectively.

TABLE III. ACCURACY OF THE CONSIDERED POSITIONING SYSTEMS

	Marvelmind	HTC VIVE	Pozyx	Aruco
Accuracy (mean) [mm]	19,62	8,05	150,73	99,15
Accuracy (P95) [mm]	33,28	12,62	283,21	177,09

A. Marvelmind

Figure 4 shows the Marvelmind positioning results together with the ground truth reference. It is clear that both trajectories are a close match. At certain sections it can be challenging to distinguish the two from one another. The mean accuracy with respect to the ground truth reference is 19,62 mm. The 95% interval of the cumulative error distribution was determined to be 33,28 mm. Therefore, it appears that the advertised accuracy of 2 cm is consistent with the average observed accuracy. However, it should be noted that the CMM has a relatively limited measurement range (as can be seen in Figure 4). When performing experiments in larger space, there inexplicably exists a region where the Marvelmind system does not measure at all. We were unable to determine the cause of this signal loss, as the beacons were not obstructed in this space nor were there any apparent sources of interference present.

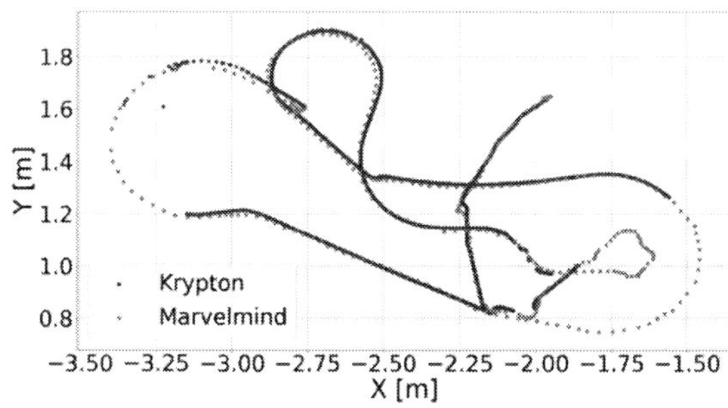

Figure 4. Marvelmind positioning results alongside Krypton CMM measurements.

B. Pozyx

The Pozyx beacons were placed at an equal height in an approximate square. In order to improve accuracy, the distances between the beacons were determined based on manual measurements rather than using the self-calibration function (this is also recommended in the documentation [16]). The relative distances can be used to calculate the angles of the approximate square (see Figure 5), these angles should then sum to 360 degrees. If this is the case, the beacon angles and distances can be used to determine the beacon locations in any coordinate system. In this paper, one beacon is selected as the origin, and the other beacons are defined relative to it.

Positioning results were not as expected. The large degree of noise in positioning data means determining the best fit is challenging. When a fit is possible, positioning errors are on average around 150 mm, with a P95 value of 233 mm (see Figure 6). These results can likely be attributed to the large amounts of metal present in the lab environment, which reduces the accuracy of UWB ranging. Therefore, a measurement was also performed with a static receiver in an open outdoor area. The results of this experiment are shown in Figure 7. The measured positions are spread over an area of approximately 20 cm, thus implying that the maximum (static) accuracy of the system is 10 cm.

Our results are slightly better than the evaluation in [10], where a mean accuracy of 20 cm was obtained. However, a P95 value was not specified. Our analysis reaches significantly different results than those in [9]. However, we suspect the authors may have used a different definition for accuracy. Negative values for 3D accuracy are present in some of the figures, which is impossible in the definition in (2). The definition that the authors did use is not specified. The obtained mean accuracy is significantly better than that of the DecaWave kit benchmarking in [6]. Additionally, our obtained P95 value is much better than even the 90% interval measured by the authors. Since the Pozyx developers kit used in this paper makes use of DecaWave transceivers, we can therefore conclude that their additions such as machine learning and sensor fusion improve performance, particularly at high intervals of the cumulative probability function.

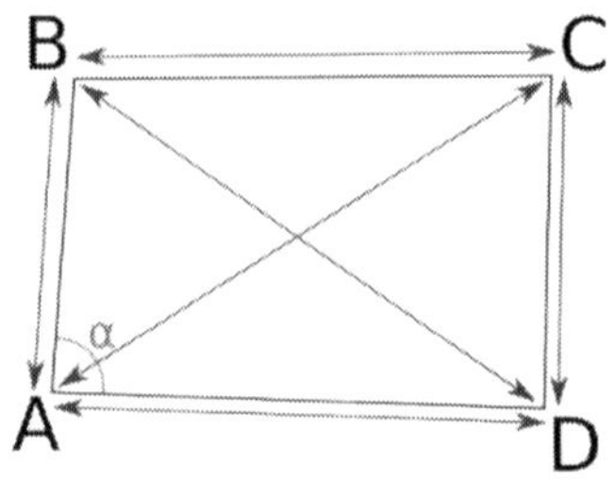

Figure 5. Calibration of Pozyx beacon positions

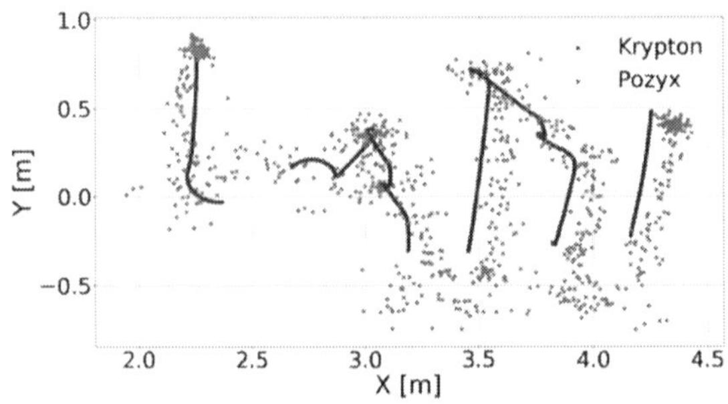

Figure 6. Pozyx positioning results (red) alongside Krypton CMM measurements (blue).

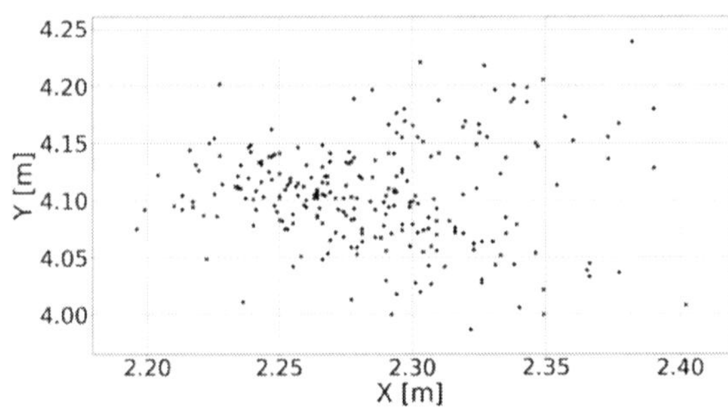

Figure 7. Reported positions by pozyx when the receiver remains static in an outdoor environment. Beacons were placed approximately 5 meters apart.

C. *Aruco marker tracking*

Positioning results from the computer vision system show significantly less noise than the Pozyx system. Accuracy is relatively high in the center of the test space. However, this accuracy decreases towards the edge of the image (see Figure 8), possibly due to a small degree of image distortion that remains even after calibration. Accuracy relative to the krypton ground truth is around 100 mm on average, with a P95 value of 177 mm.

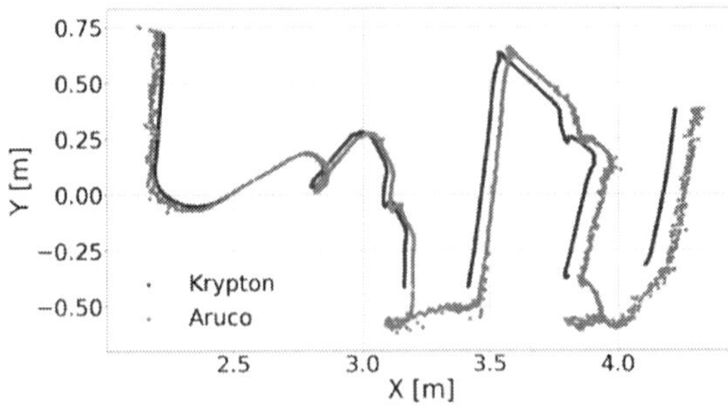

Figure 8. Camera positioning results (red) alongside Krypton CMM measurements (blue). Data was fitted to the left side of the figure, which is why deviation is smallest in this region. Evaluation is performed on the rest of the dataset which was not fitted.

D. *HTC VIVE tracker*

The HTC VIVE proves to be the most accurate system out of all the experiments. As can be seen on Figure 9, the two datasets match very closely, in fact it is challenging to observe any difference. Therefore, these results are also shown in a different perspective in Figure 10. Small variations in the z-coordinate of the reference system are present. These variations can likely be attributed to a non-perfect smoothness of the floor or roundness of the robot wheels. The average positioning error relative to the ground truth is 8 mm, with a P95 value of 12 mm.

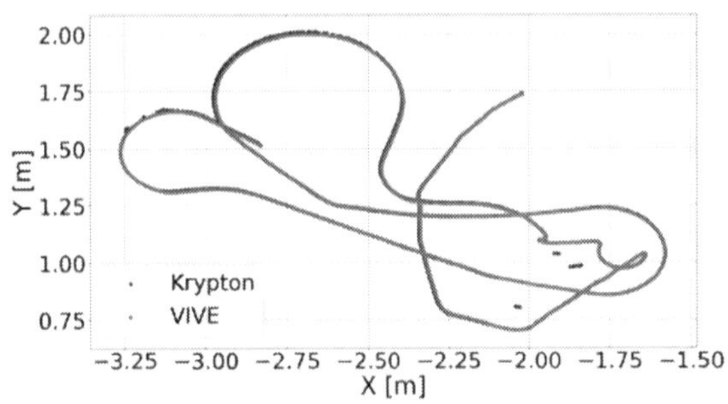

Figure 9. HTC VIVE positioning results (red) alongside Krypton CMM measurements (blue).

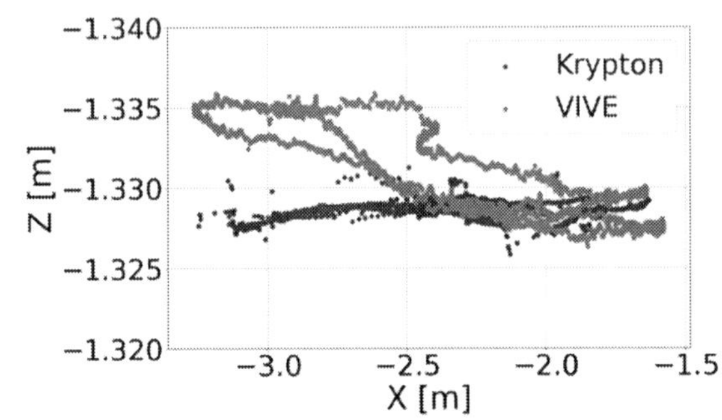

Figure 10. Side view of the HTC VIVE positioning results (red) alongside the Krypton CMM measurements (blue)

VI. Conclusion

In this paper, we benchmarked a number of low-cost indoor positioning systems. We used a highly accurate reference system rather than conventional grid measurements or measurements with a ruler as a ground truth. Additionally, we measure the ground truth position at a high rate to better characterize dynamic performance. While there likely will never be a single 'best' indoor positioning system, it is clear from our results that significant progress has been made in recent years. For just a few hundred euros, it is now possible to purchase a positioning system that delivers accuracy of a few centimeters out of the box. If one has more technical expertise, then the HTC VIVE can provide even higher accuracy. It is even possible to use the VIVE as a ground truth reference for positioning systems that have an accuracy that is one order of magnitude less than 1 cm. In this case, the VIVE can be a more interesting option than the krypton CMM due the drastic reduction in cost and the larger measurement space. When a very low-cost positioning solution is required, it is possible to achieve, on average, sub-decimeter accuracy for the price of an webcam. However, both the HTC VIVE and the camera based solution do not scale to larger environments, unlike for the Marvelmind or Pozyx systems.

Future work can extend this analysis to include more positioning systems. For example by including commercially available optical tracking systems. Additional performance metrics such as precision and power use could also be evaluated, to provide a more complete assessment of the IPS. Finally, the experiments in this paper were performed at approximately the same movement speed. An evaluation at a range of velocities could be useful for highly dynamic applications (e.g., drones).

Acknowledgment

Robin Amsters is an SB fellow of the Research Foundation Flanders (FWO) under grant agreement 1S57718N.

References

[1] L. Mainetti, L. Patrono, and I. Sergi, "A survey on indoor positioning systems," in 2014 22nd International Conference on Software, Telecommunications and Computer Networks, SoftCOM 2014. IEEE, sep 2014, pp. 111–120. [Online]. Available: http://ieeexplore.ieee.org/lpdocs/epic03/wrapper.htm?arnumber=7039067

[2] N. E. Klepeis et al., "National Human Activity Pattern Survey (NHAPS): Use of nationwide activity data for human exposure assessment The National Human Activity Pattern Survey (NHAPS): a resource for assessing exposure to environmental pollutants," Journal of exposure analysis and environmental epidemiology, 2001, pp. 231–252.

[3] P. Connolly and D. Bonte, "Indoor Location in Retail: Where is the Money?" ABI Research, Tech. Rep., 2016, URL: https://www.abiresearch.com/market-research/product/1025355-indoor-location-in-retail-where-is-the-mon/ [accessed: 2018-12-21].

[4] R. Mautz, "Indoor Positioning Technologies," Habilitation thesis, ETH Zurich, 2012, URL: http://e-collection.library.ethz.ch/eserv/eth:5659/eth-5659-01.pdf [accessed: 2018-12-21].

[5] T. Van Haute et al., "Performance analysis of multiple Indoor Positioning Systems in a healthcare environment," International Journal of Health Geographics, vol. 15, no. 1, 2016, p. 7.

[6] A. Jimenez and F. Seco, "Comparing Decawave and Bespoon UWB location systems: Indoor/outdoor performance analysis," in 2016 International Conference on Indoor Positioning and Indoor Navigation (IPIN), vol. 66, no. 8. IEEE, oct 2016, pp. 1–8, URL: http://ieeexplore.ieee.org/document/7743686/ [accessed: 2018-12-21].

[7] A. R. J. Ruiz and F. S. Granja, "Comparing Ubisense, BeSpoon, and DecaWave UWB Location Systems: Indoor Performance Analysis," IEEE Transactions on Instrumentation and Measurement, vol. 66, no. 8, 2017, pp. 2106–2117.

[8] R. Maalek and F. Sadeghpour, "Accuracy assessment of ultra-wide band technology in locating dynamic resources in indoor scenarios," Automation in Construction, vol. 63, 2016, pp. 12–26. [Online]. Available: http://dx.doi.org/10.1016/j.autcon.2015.11.009

[9] P. Dabove, V. Di Pietra, M. Piras, A. A. Jabbar, and S. A. Kazim, "Indoor positioning using Ultra-wide band (UWB) technologies: Positioning accuracies and sensors' performances," 2018 IEEE/ION Position, Location and Navigation Symposium, PLANS 2018 - Proceedings, 2018, pp. 175–184.

[10] M. Ridolfi et al., "Experimental evaluation of uwb indoor positioning for sport postures," Sensors (Switzerland), vol. 18, no. 1, 2018, pp. 1–20.

[11] J. Cernohorský and M. Novák, "Mobile robot indoor navigation," 2016, pp. 151–155.

[12] C.-M. Chang, C.-H. Hsu, C.-F. Hsu, and K.-T. Chen, "Performance Measurements of Virtual Reality Systems: Quantifying the Timing and Positioning Accuracy," Proceedings of the 2016 ACM on Multimedia Conference - MM '16, 2016, pp. 655–659. [Online]. Available: http://dl.acm.org/citation.cfm?doid=2964284.2967303

[13] D. C. Niehorster, L. Li, and M. Lappe, "The accuracy and precision of position and orientation tracking in the HTC vive virtual reality system for scientific research," i-Perception, vol. 8, no. 3, 2017, pp. 1–23.

[14] S. Adler, S. Schmitt, K. Wolter, and M. Kyas, "A survey of experimental evaluation in indoor localization research," Indoor Positioning and Indoor Navigation (IPIN), 2015 International Conference on, no. October, 2015, pp. 1–10.

[15] S. Gezici et al., "Localization via ultra-wideband radios a look at positioning aspects for future sensor networks," IEEE Signal Processing Magazine, vol. 22, no. 4, 2005, pp. 70–84.

[16] Pozyx Labs, "Pozyx - centimeter positioning for arduino," 2015, URL: https://www.pozyx.io/Documentation/Tutorials/ready_to_localize [accessed: 2018-09-11].

[17] Valve, "VIVE - Vive Tracker," 2017, URL: https://www.vive.com/us/vive-tracker/ [accessed: 2018-09-11].

[18] O. Kreylos, "Lighthouse tracking examined — Doc-Ok.org," 2016, URL: http://doc-ok.org/?p=1478 [accessed: 2018-09-10].

[19] J. Van den Heuvel, "Driver Documentation," 2018, URL: https://github.com/ValveSoftware/openvr/wiki/Driver-Documentation [accessed: 2018-12-21].

[20] S. Garrido-Jurado, R. Muñoz-Salinas, F. J. Madrid-Cuevas, and M. J. Marín-Jiménez, "Automatic generation and detection of highly reliable fiducial markers under occlusion," Pattern Recognition, vol. 47, no. 6, jun 2014, pp. 2280–2292. [Online]. Available: http://linkinghub.elsevier.com/retrieve/pii/S0031320314000235

[21] OpenCV, "Camera calibration With OpenCV OpenCV 2.4.13.7 documentation," 2014, URL: https://docs.opencv.org/2.4/doc/tutorials/calib3d/camera{_}calibration/camera{_}calibration.html [accessed: 2018-09-11].

[22] Krypton Electronic Engineering n.v., "Krypton Help Pages on K400/K600 Hardware & Software Guide," Leuven, Tech. Rep., 2003. [Online]. Available: http://nees.buffalo.edu/training/krypton/kx00_manual_EN.PDF

[23] J. C. Gower, "Generalized procrustes analysis," Psychometrika, vol. 40, no. 1, 1975, pp. 33–51. [Online]. Available: https://doi.org/10.1007/BF02291478

[24] W. Kabsch, "A solution for the best rotation to relate two sets of vectors," Acta Crystallographica Section A, vol. 32, no. 5, sep 1976, pp. 922–923. [Online]. Available: https://doi.org/10.1107/S0567739476001873

Low-Cost Optical System for Pressure Measurements Within a Combustion Chamber of an Internal Combustion Engine

Jernej Hribar
Laboratory for Electro Optics and Sensory Systems
Faculty of Electrical Engineering and Computer Science
Maribor, Slovenia
e-mail: jernej.hribar@um.si

Boris Macuh
Laboratory for Electro Optics and Sensory Systems
Faculty of Electrical Engineering and Computer Science
Maribor, Slovenia
e-mail: boris.macuh@um.si

Prof. Dr. Dušan Gleich
Laboratory for Signal Processing and Remote Control
Faculty of Electrical Engineering and Computer Science
Maribor, Slovenia
dusan.gleich@um.si

Prof. Dr. Denis Đonlagić
Laboratory for Electro Optics and Sensory Systems
Faculty of Electrical Engineering and Computer Science
Maribor, Slovenia
denis.donlagic@um.si

Abstract— **This contribution presents a novel low-cost approach to interrogation of short cavity Fabry-Perot optical fiber sensors and their use for pressure measurements in a combustion chamber of a petrol or diesel engine. The optical fiber sensor interrogation system is based on laser diodes with different wavelengths. Reflectance from Fabry-Perot sensors at three different wavelengths was observed to determine the cavity length, using specially developed signal processing algorithms. The interrogation system was evaluated statically and dynamically. It is shown that the interrogation system has a resolution of about 2 nm and bandwidth of 16 kHz. Two sensor designs were studied and evaluated in both the laboratory environment and in a combustion chamber of the engine. Both sensor designs are executed on the tip of the optical fiber, with etching, cleaving and splicing of special optical fibers.**

Keywords—Low-cost interrogator; optical fiber sensor; pressure measurement; internal combustion engine; signal processing algorithm

I. Introduction

Stricter ecological demands from the authorities and lower fuel consumption demands from the consumers of the cars with Internal Combustion Engines (ICE) are forcing the automotive industry into development and production of more efficient engines with lower emissions in the environment [1]. Research in both academia and industry is focused to achieve those goals [1]-[4], with, but not limited to: Downsizing of the engines, supercharging, variable controlled valves, novel fuels or their mixtures, etc. An important part of ICE are their sensors; information from them serves the electronic control unit for optimization of combustion and, consequently, lowering both consumption and emissions. In-cylinder pressure sensors have been investigated for a few decades, due to the rich nature of information that we can extract from the pressure curve. But, even after decades of research, the design of a low-cost pressure sensor, which would fulfil the price requirements of the automotive industry to implement it in the low and mid cost series production cars, which are responsible for a large part of global emissions, proved to be challenging. On the other hand, optical fiber sensors are known for their durability and reliability in harsh environments. Very often, they offer superior properties in terms of resolution and speed. Optical fiber sensors are connected to an interrogation unit, which is responsible for conversion of the measured parameter to a desired output, and is, as much as the sensors, responsible for the properties of the optical fiber measurement system. Commonly, the interrogation unit represents the bigger part of the cost of the optical fiber sensor system, and, due to its cost, optical fiber sensors have not made a breakthrough in consumer applications.

We present a new, low-cost method to interrogate a short cavity optical fiber Fabry-Perot (FP) sensor. While most of the reliable methods for interrogation of fiber FP sensors are based on wavelength sweep or wavelength filtering, our approach is based on only three different wavelengths. FP optical fiber sensors are involved in Metrology due to their low cost of production and a wide range of possible uses [5].

In Section 2 the theoretical background of the interrogation system will be presented, followed by the physical configuration of the system in Section 3. Section 4 will provide a short program description. Sensor mounting will be presented in section 5, followed by Results and Discussion in Section 6. Finally, in Section 7, conclusions and further work will be presented.

II. Theoretical Background of the Interrogation System

Interrogation of FP optical fiber sensors is a well-known problem, which is solved mainly with expensive equipment, inappropriate for our application. Most of them are based on a wavelength tuneable source or optical spectral analyzer. If we measure the wavelength response of an FP sensor, we get a "lifted sinusoid" response, from which we can determine with great accuracy the length of the interferometer. Our approach is based on three laser diodes with different wavelengths. We measure sensors` reflectance at different wavelengths with a photodiode, which is given by (1).

$$y_1 = A\left(1 + Bcos4\pi\frac{L}{\lambda_1}\right)$$

$$y_2 = A\left(1 + Bcos4\pi\frac{L}{\lambda_2}\right) \quad (1)$$

$$y_3 = A\left(1 + Bcos4\pi\frac{L}{\lambda_3}\right)$$

y_x – response from a given wavelength
A – amplitude of the sinusoid
B – offset of the sinusoid
L – length of the FP cavity
λ_x – wavelength of the given laser diode

Solving (1) gives us (2) and (3) which are solutions for A, B:

$$A = \frac{y_1}{1 + Bcos4\pi\frac{L}{\lambda_1}} \quad (2)$$

$$B = \frac{y_1 - y_2}{y_2cos4\pi\frac{L}{\lambda_1} - y_1cos4\pi\frac{L}{\lambda_2}} \quad (3)$$

The length of the FP cavity is calculated with Newton's gradient method as seen in (4) and (5).

$$F(L) = k\left(cos4\pi\frac{L}{\lambda_1} - cos4\pi\frac{L}{\lambda_3}\right) - \left(cos4\pi\frac{L}{\lambda_1} - cos4\pi\frac{L}{\lambda_2}\right) \quad (4)$$

$$L_k = L_{K-1} - F(L)/F(L)' \quad (5)$$

For known wavelengths of the laser diodes, we can calculate the length of the FP interferometer.

III. PHYSICAL CONFIGURATION OF THE PROPOSED SYSTEM

The electro-optical configuration of the proposed interrogation system is presented in Figure 1. The system is built around a specially designed optical module consisting of three Fabry-Perot laser diodes, packed in a housing with optical elements providing good coupling into an SM fiber. The optical fiber is connected to the 50:50 2X2 optical fiber coupler, which splits the light into two equivalent parts. One part of the light goes to the photodetector for monitoring transmitted light, and the second goes to the sensor, which reflects some of the light back to the coupler. Half of the reflected light goes back to laser diodes and is lost, the other half goes to the second photo diode for monitoring reflected light.

The electronic part of the system is based on a microcontroller (PIC 32MZ family), which controls all the components described below. The design must provide us with sequential powering of the laser diodes with adjustable current. This is achieved with three equal electronic circuits consisting of a digital potentiometer, voltage buffer, digital switch, and a current driver with mosfet transistor. Such layout enables serial switching of the laser diodes on and off in the range of tens of microseconds. The detector side consists of two standard optical fiber coupled photodiodes and transimpedance

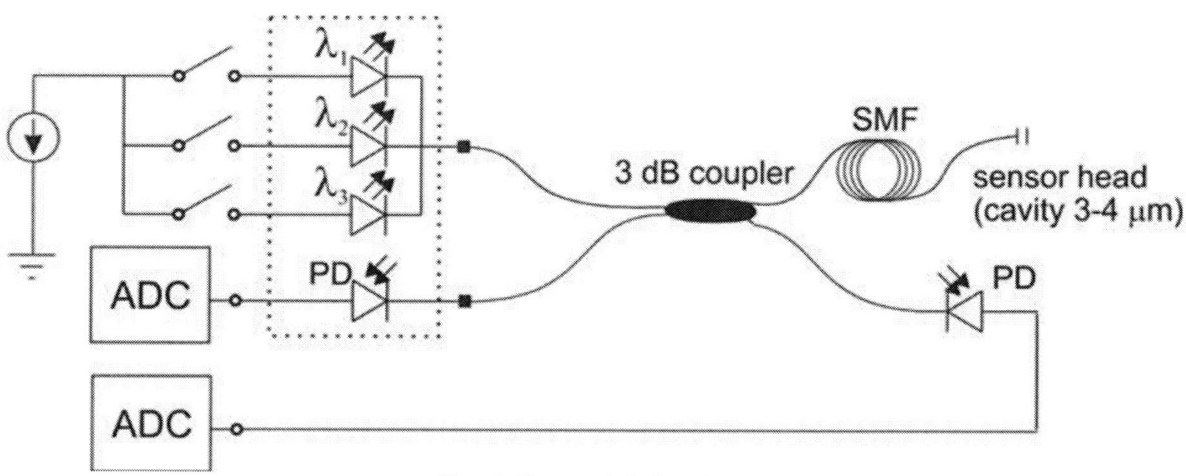

Figure 1: Electro- optical schematic

amplifiers with gains of 87 thousand and 2 million, for measuring the transmitted light and reflected light from the sensor, respectively. Signals from the amplifiers are routed to the microcontrollers` AD converter pins.

Two types of optical fiber pressure sensors are considered, both micromachined on the top of the standard SM optical fiber. First is the so-called needle sensor [6], as depicted in Figure 3 (b). The needle sensor was initially meant for strain measurements. Responsivity of a needle sensor with a 400 μm long gutter is about 2 nm/bar. Its production process is appropriate for massive production and, therefore, the needle is our first choice. The second sensor is a membrane pressure sensor [7], Figure 3 (a) . Its production process is more complex, but design of the structure is better, because it`s similar to some classical pressure sensors. Also, the responsivity can be set individually during the production process.

IV. SHORT PROGRAM DESCRIPTION

The program is a crucial part of the whole system because it must run fast enough to provide enough throughput of the whole system. Stable timing is achieved with timers and interrupts. Four switching states are implemented, as depicted in Figure 2, three for when each laser diode is turned on, and one when all diodes are turned off and we measure the dark optical power. This had to be implemented due to the optical power from combustion coupling into the fiber. Proper timing of the analog-digital conversion is also ensured with timers and interrupts. After all samples are taken, we start the algorithm for calculation of the length of the FP cavity. First, results are averaged with the number of samples taken in one state. After that they are "normalized". Responses have undesired offsets and different amplitudes for different wavelengths, therefore, we must normalize all the signals to an even interval throughout the complete measuring range for all three wavelengths. Finally, we use equations 4 and 5 to determine the length of the cavity. With measured length of the cavity, responsivity of the sensor and initial length of the cavity, we calculate the pressure.

V. SENSOR MOUNTING

We designed a similar insert to the industry standard probe for measuring pressure in the combustion chamber (from the company AVL LIST GmbH). Redesigned and finished sensors are depicted in Figure 4. Bonding of fiber to the insert has proven to be difficult due to the high temperatures and pressures. Primarily, tests with two component epoxy adhesives were executed, but under high pressures the sensor fiber

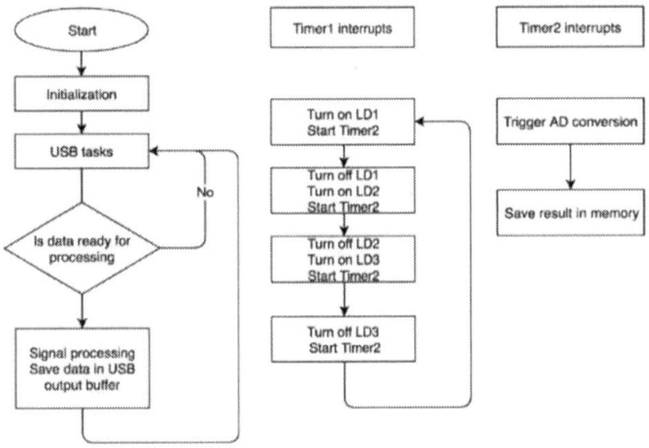

Figure 2: Program's flow chart

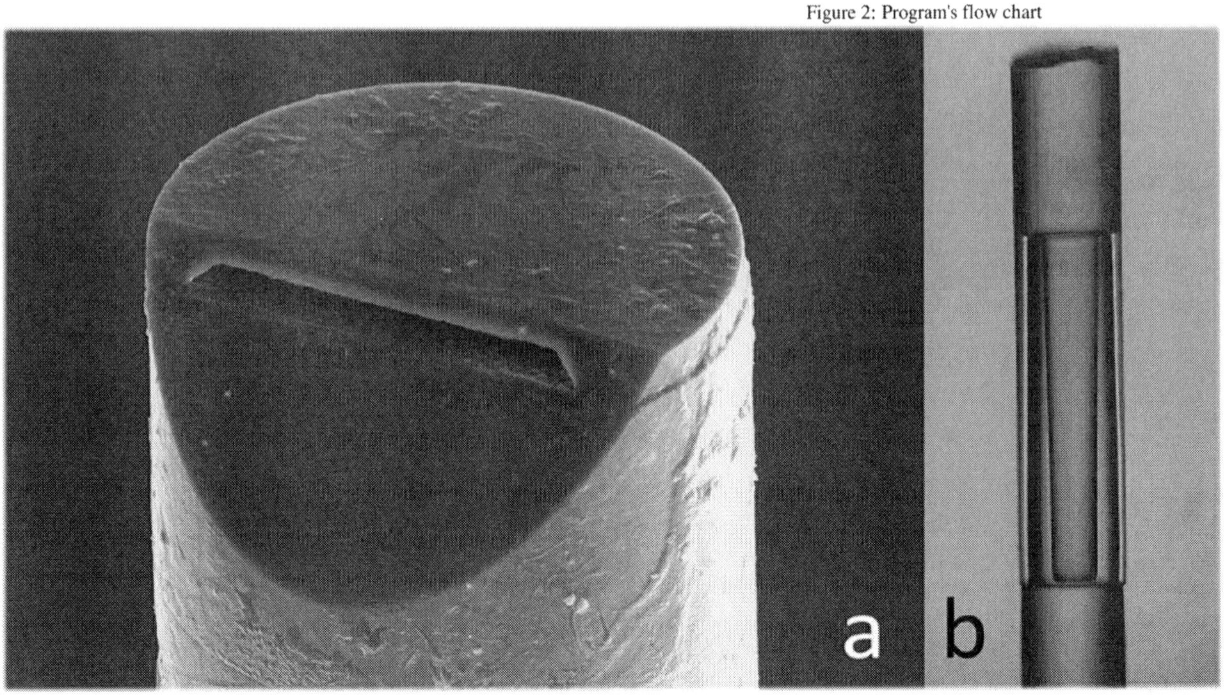

Figure 3: (a) Section view of membrane sensor (SEM), (b) Needle sensor (optical microscope), diameter of both is 125 μm

was excreted. Excretion was solved with usage of EPO-TEK 353ND. This joint has proven to be suitable for temperatures up to 350°C.

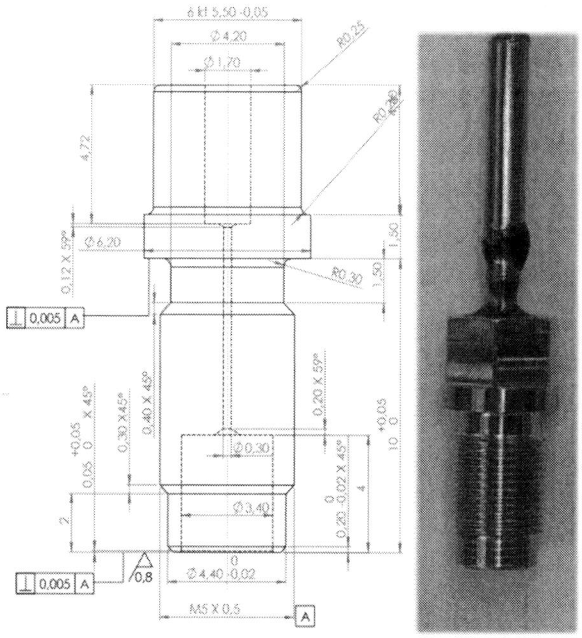

Figure 4: Redesigned insert for pressure measurement and finished insert

VI. RESULTS AND DISCUSSION

The interrogation system was evaluated in laboratory conditions under both static and dynamic conditions. Static testing was performed with a needle sensor being stretched. The sensor forming fiber was left long enough to glue it to a linear stage, while the lead in fiber was glued to a stationary block of aluminum. The aluminum block and linear stage were secured on the optical table with screws. With moving of the linear stage, we got the results from the interrogation system given in the following graph. As seen in Figure 5, the interrogation system has a very good linearity over an almost 1 micrometre span.

Dynamic testing was performed with the needle sensor glued to a PZT stack. The PZT stack was excited with a 140 Hz square signal.As seen in Figure 6, 2, nanometres of noise are presented at 16 kHz sampling, considering the typical sensitivity of the membrane sensor we achieved noise of 500 mbar.After validation of the interrogation system, tests in the engine followed.

Test were performed on a Toyota 4Y ECS engine, fuelled with natural gas. This type of engine was developed for industrial forklifts. The engine was mounted on the test bench and coupled with an engine brake. We tested under different brake torques: 45 Nm, 100Nm and 115 Nm. Engine speed was 1500 rpm. The pressure curve acquired with the needle sensor is partially valid only during periods of high pressure, but in the periods of gas exchange, it is very distorted, due to rapid temperature changes, as the outer side of the structure got heated more than the inner pedestal. Therefore, false readings of pressure were acquired due to the uneven thermal expansion of the complete structure. Additionally, we had some difficulties with vibrations on the needle sensor due to high frequency vibrations introduced by the engine, so we needed

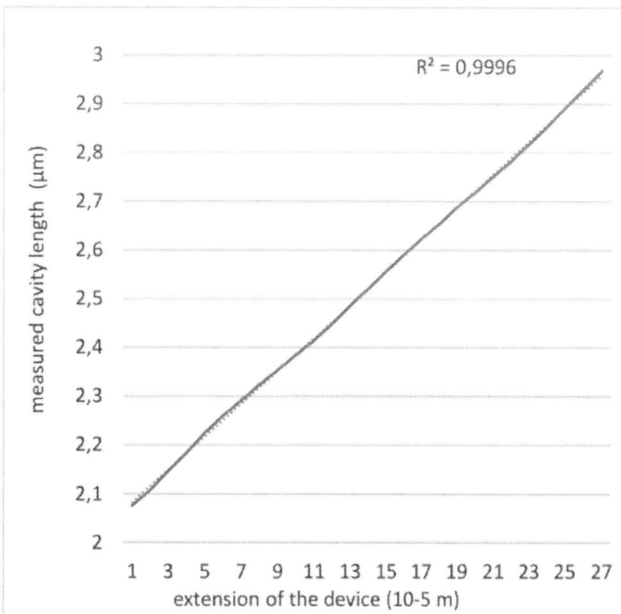

Figure 5: Linear response of the interrogation system

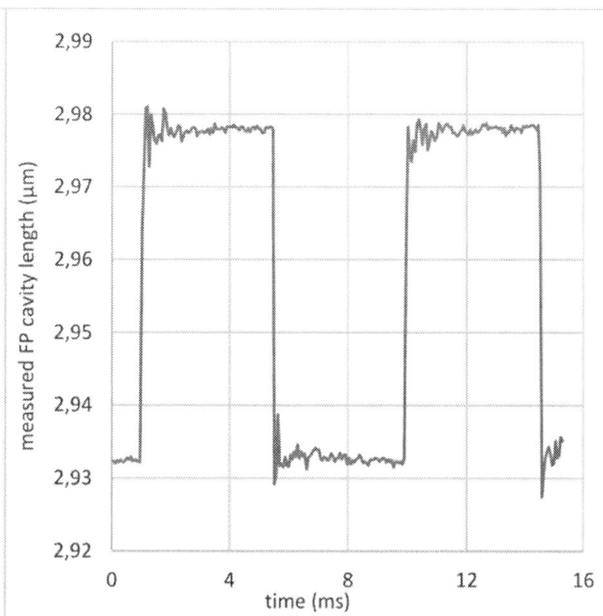

Figure 6: Dynamic response of the interrogation system

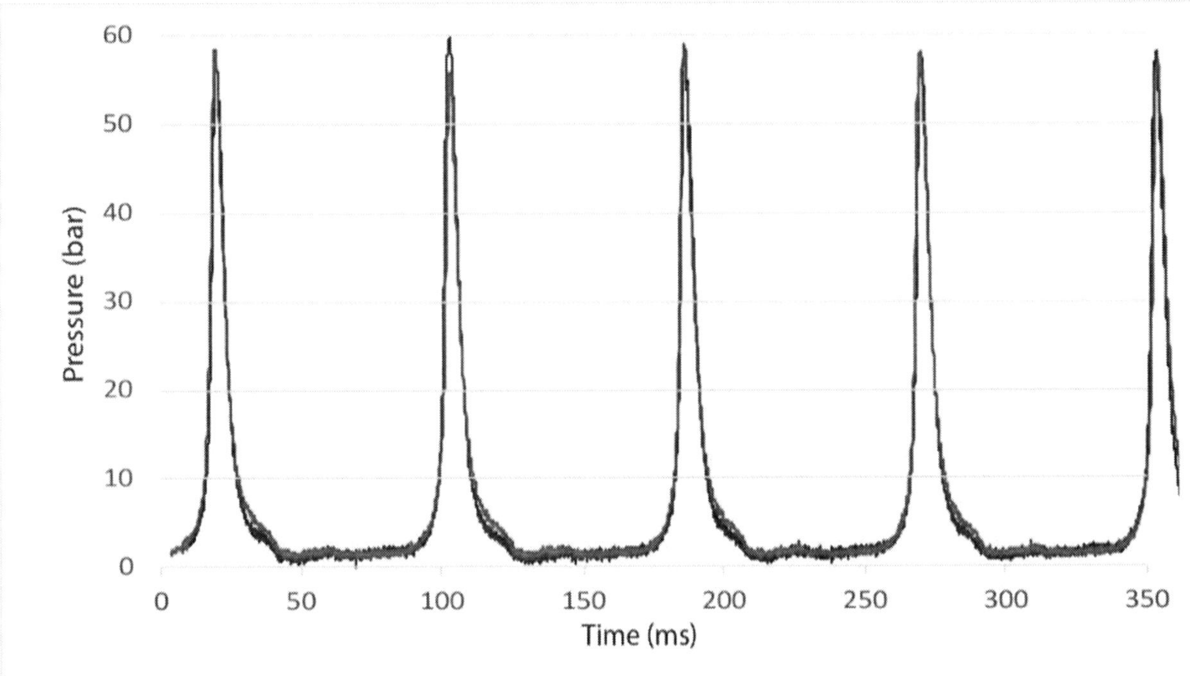

Figure 7: Pressure curves under work conditions at 1500 rpm and 115Nm braking torque. The red curve is measured with the proposed system, the black curve is a reference, measured with an AVL probe

to set the distance between the epoxy adhesive and the structure to such a length that those effects were minimized.

The following is the pressure measured with the membrane sensor after it has been inserted in the combustion chamber for 100 working hours. It has been observed that sensors do not age in this time period. The pressure curve in Figure 7 is valid throughout the complete combustion cycle.

VII. Conclusion and Further Work

This paper presented a low-cost interrogation system with corresponding sensors for pressure measurements under extreme conditions of a combustion chamber in automotive applications. Simple construction of the complete system and, therefore, minimum components, are used to achieve low cost design with good reliability.

The system was tested both under laboratory conditions and in a real engine. Resolution of 2 nm was shown, which matches 0.5 bar.

At the time, commercially available pressure sensors for combustion chambers were developed and manufactured by the company AVL LIST GmbH, for example GH15D, but, due to different approaches of measurement, additional work must be done in the direction of maturing of our solution. Further work must be done into research of dynamic temperature changes on the needle sensor to minimise those undesirable effects.

Acknowledgment

This work was part of the project »Ecological Safe Vehicle for green mobility - EVA4green« is co-financed by the Republic of Slovenia and the European Union under the European Regional Development Fund«, it was also supported by the Slovenian Research Agency as part of the Young Researcher program.

References

[1] P. Brijesh and S. Sreedhara, "Exhaust Emissions and Its Control Methods in Compression Ignition Engines: A Review," International Journal of Automotive Technology, vol. 14, no. 2, pp. 195-206, Apr 2013, doi:10.1007/s12239-013-0022-2.

[2] T. A. Parlikar et al., "Design and experimental implementation of an electromagnetic engine valve drive," Ieee-Asme Transactions on Mechatronics, vol. 10, no. 5, pp. 482-494, Oct 2005, doi:10.1109/Tmech.2005.856221.

[3] A. M. K. P. Taylor, "Science review of internal combustion engines," Energy Policy, vol. 36, no. 12, pp. 4657-4667, Dec 2008, doi:10.1016/j.enpol.2008.09.001.

[4] D. T. Zhu and X. Q. Zheng, "A new asymmetric twin-scroll turbine with two wastegates for energy improvements in diesel engines," Applied Energy, vol. 223, pp. 263-272, Aug 2018, doi:10.1016/j.apenergy.2018.04.078.

[5] M. R. Islam, M. M. Ali, M. H. Lai, K. S. Lim, and H. Ahmad, "Chronology of Fabry-Perot Interferometer Fiber-Optic Sensors and Their Applications: A Review," Sensors, vol. 14, no. 4, pp. 7451-7488, Apr 2014. doi:10.3390/s140407451.

[6] S. Pevec and D. Donlagic, "All-fiber, long-active-length Fabry-Perot strain sensor," Optics Express, vol. 19, no. 16, pp. 15641-15651, Aug 2011, doi: 10.1364/Oe.19.015641.

[7] D. Donlagic and E. Cibula, "All-fiber high-sensitivity pressure sensor with SiO2 diaphragm," Optics Letters, vol. 30, no. 16, pp. 2071-2073, Aug 2005, doi:10.1364/OL.30.002071.

Testing of a Developed Multigas Sensor System for Outdoor Odour Nuisance Monitoring

Michael Hofmann, Carlo Tiebe
8.1 Sensors, Measurement and Testing Methods
Bundesanstalt für Materialforschung und -prüfung (BAM)
Berlin, Germany
e-mail: michael.hofmann@bam.de, carlo.tiebe@bam.de

Mohammed Moufid, Nezha El Bari, Benachir Bouchikhi
Laboratory of Electronic Automatic and Biotechnology
Faculty of Sciences, Moulay Ismaïl University,
Meknes, Morocco
e-mail: mohammed.moufid.2@gmail.com,
n_elbari@hotmail.com, benachir.bouchikhi@gmail.com

***Abstract*—This work presents the testing of a developed electronic nose for outdoor odour nuisance monitoring. The sensor system consists of a sampling system, a measuring cell equipped with commercially available low-cost gas sensor elements and a data acquisition system. The sensor testing showed that the developed prototype is able to distinguish, identify and partially quantify individual odorous substances like ethanol, ammonia and hydrogen sulphide. Ethanol and ammonia could even be detected below or near their odour threshold.**

Keywords-electronic nose; outdoor odour; machined olfaction; sensor testing.

I. Introduction

Odour nuisances in outdoor air, e.g., caused by emissions from industrial or agricultural facilities into the environment, can seriously affect the well-being and health of residents. For the detection and evaluation of the outdoor odour immission, i.e. at a point of exposure to the residents, olfactometric methods exist, which are based on the human sensory perception of trained examinants forming a so-called qualified panel [1][2]. However, the relevance and the degree of odour nuisances are often difficult to assess, as they are only recorded and evaluated by persons with individual subjective olfactory perception, in a short time interval and in a limited spatial resolution. Therefore, olfactory measurements, even though performed with trained examiners, are subject to considerable standard deviations and measurement uncertainties. The application of an objective sensor-supported measurement method - machined olfaction - as a supporting and complementary method is consequently of great interest.

In a Moroccan-German research project, such a tool in the form of a multi-gas sensor system, also known as an electronic nose, shall be developed and tested under laboratory and field conditions. In addition, measurement strategies for odour monitoring in the outdoor air are to be derived from the tests.

This paper presents the results of a proficiency test of the developed prototype under laboratory conditions for a selection of odorants and is organised as follows. In section II the used materials and methods are described. Section III obtained results are presented and discussed. Conclusions of the investigations are given in section IV.

II. Materials and Methods

A. Electronic Nose

The prototype of the electronic nose [3] consists of a 270 cm^3 measuring cell equipped with six commercially available solid-state metal oxide semiconductor gas sensor elements (MQ-3, -4, -5, -8, -9, -135, Winsen Electronics Technology Co., Ltd, Zhengzhou, China) for the differentiation, identification and quantification of gaseous substances, as well as a temperature (LM35DZ, Texas Instruments, Dallas, USA) and a relative humidity sensor (HIH 4000, Honeywell International Inc., Morristown, USA). For data acquisition, a multifunction data I/O device (NI USB-6212, National Instruments, Austin, USA) with 16 bit analog to digital converters is employed, which transfers the data to a PC running a LabVIEW graphical user interface. Sampling can be performed either indirectly via a micro pump and 2 dm^3 Tedlar® bags (TB) or directly at a gas flow rate of 250 cm^3 min^{-1}.

B. Feature extraction and pattern recognition

To derive evaluable information from the complex sensor responses of the electronic nose, characteristic features were extracted from the measurement signals of each gas sensor. These are: the initial conductance (G_0), the steady-state conductance (G_S), the dynamic slope of the conductance (dG/dt) and the area under curve (A). Based on these features, a Principal Component Analysis (PCA) was performed for dimension reduction.

C. Test gas generation

For sensor testing, the Gas Mixing System (GMS) of the accredited test laboratory for the testing of sensors for determining the composition of non-explosive gas mixtures of BAM was used. The method bases on dilution of gas streams. The traceability is given by the usage of certified test gases from gas cylinders, calibrated thermal mass flow controllers into a zero-gas stream of known composition. In addition, volatile organic compounds (VOC) or volatile inorganic compounds can be added traceable to the mass into the gas stream via a liquid evaporator or a permeator.

D. Sensor testing

The basic requirements for the behaviour of the employed sensor elements were tested by exposure to individual test gases from gas cylinders containing:

- Ethanol with a volume fraction of 483 cm^3 m^{-3} (ppm),
- Ammonia with a volume fraction of 28.86 ppm and
- Hydrogen sulphide with a volume fraction of 11.13 ppm

in synthetic air. Different volume fractions were adjusted with the GMS of BAM by adjusting the mixing ratio. Sampling was performed both indirectly via TB and directly from the test gas stream (without the micro pump).

In the further course of the sensor testing, the response to a mixture of the mentioned test gases, artificial odour of a pig farm, which is commercially available as "PigOdour" (Olfasense, Kiel, Germany), and components identified via Gas Chromatography–Mass Spectrometry (GC-MS) from outdoor odour samples in morocco collected by Tenax® TA filled thermal desorption (TD) tubes are tested under variable climatic conditions. After passing the laboratory tests, the performance of the electronic nose is tested in the field.

III. RESULTS AND DISCUSSION

Figure 1 shows the PCA plot resulting from the extracted feature datasets of the measurements of ethanol, ammonia (NH_3) and hydrogen sulphide (H_2S) for indirect (a) and direct sampling (b) together with the blank value of the corresponding sampling system.

For indirect sampling, the cluster of the blank value measurement overlaps with the odorant measurements in the lower volume fraction range (3 ppm of ethanol, 7.3 ppm of NH_3 and 0.1 ppm as well as 1 ppm of H_2S). The measurements of the remaining test gas concentrations could be well separated by PCA.

With direct sampling, a better separation of the clusters is achieved than with indirect sampling. Only the clusters of the blank value measurement overlap with the measurements of 0.1 ppm and 1 ppm of H_2S.

Especially at low odorant concentrations as it is to be found in outdoor air, the use of TB is only suitable to a limited extent since the material act both as a sink and, in the case of inadequate cleaning, as a source of VOC. In this study, *N,N*-dimethylacetamide and phenol were determined as main contaminants of the TB via TD GC-MS.

IV. CONCLUSION

This paper describes the need for traceable test gas generation methods for testing of this developed multi gas sensor device (electronic nose).

With very simple and cost-effective gas sensors, which are applicable in products for citizen science, it is possible to differentiate, identify and partially quantify odorous substances with good discrimination strength within short measuring times.

For the considered outdoor air application, a direct sampling and thus a portable measuring device is essential. A corresponding adaptation of the measuring system is planned.

ACKNOWLEDGMENT

This work has received funding from the German Federal Ministry of Education and Research (BMBF) under grant no. 01DH16033 and Moulay Ismaïl University, Scientific Research under grant "Appui à la Recherche".

In memoriam of Dr. Thomas Hübert.

REFERENCES

[1] EN 16841-1 (2017): Ambient air - Determination of odour in ambient air by using field inspection - Part 1: Grid method, European Committee for Standardization (CEN), Brussels.

[2] EN 16841-2 (2017): Ambient air - Determination of odour in ambient air by using field inspection - Part 2: Plume method, European Committee for Standardization (CEN), Brussels.

[3] M. Moufid, C. Tiebe, N. El Bari, T. Hübert, and B. Bouchikhi, "An Electronic Nose For the Detection and Discrimination of Environmental Pollutant Gases In the Aglomeration of the City of Meknes," 8th International Workshop Biosensors for Food Safety and Environmental Monitoring, Oct. 2017, p 54.

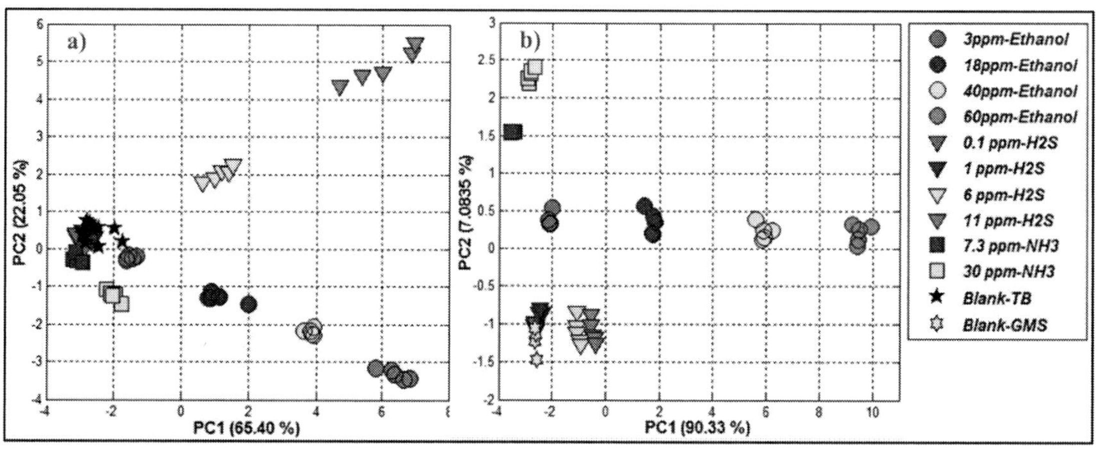

Figure 1. PCA plot performed on measurements of ethanol, H_2S and NH_3 with the electronic nose: a) indirect sampling, b) direct sampling.

Enhancing Electricity Meters with Smart Functionality Using Metering System with Optical Sensors

Mateusz Brzozowski
and Michał Kruszewski

OneMeter Ltd.
ul. Dobrzanskiego 3
20-262 Lublin, Poland
Email: {Mateusz.Brzozowski, Michal.Kruszewski}@onemeter.com

Artur Janicki

Institute of Telecommunications
Warsaw University of Technology
ul. Nowowiejska 15/19
00-665 Warsaw, Poland
OneMeter Ltd., Lublin, Poland
Email: A.Janicki@tele.pw.edu.pl

***Abstract*—The article presents on-going work on a system, called OneMeter 2.0, that uses energy-efficient beacons with optical sensors to create an advanced metering infrastructure. The system allows the use of the current, non-smart electricity meters with IEC 65056-21 optical ports to create an intelligent metering system. The core components of the system are described, such as a beacon with an optical sensor, a mobile application, and a data platform. The status of the project is presented, including the number of test installations and initial assessment of the beacon's energy efficiency. Sample visualizations originating from the data analytics platform are shown and explained.**

Keywords–Optical sensor; Beacon; Smart metering; Smart grids; AMI.

I. INTRODUCTION

In times of growing costs for electricity production and increasing problems with air pollution, the need for real-time monitoring of energy consumption is tremendous. Unsurprisingly, the European Commission requires that all member countries equip at least 80% of their electricity customers with intelligent metering systems by 2020 [1]. This is supposed to lead to the creation of smart power grids [2], which would allow for monitoring and managing of country-based and EU-based power consumption.

The process of installing smart meters is very costly and time-consuming, so it is no wonder that the majority of the EU countries, as described in the next section, are not likely to meet the above deadline. Therefore, to improve the process of deployment of smart metering, we propose a system, called OneMeter 2.0, which will use energy-efficient beacons with optical sensors, communicating via the IEC 65056-21 protocol. The system will add intelligent functionality to existing, popular, non-smart, electronic meters, called Automated Meter Reading (AMR) [3], equipped with an optical port – without a need to install smart meters at all.

In this paper, in Section II we will briefly describe the problem of smart metering deployment. Next, in Section III we will present a description of the OneMeter 2.0 system, followed by the current status of the project (Section IV). Finally, we will conclude in Section V with a plan for the future of our work.

This work was supported by the National Centre for Research and Development within the Smart Growth Operational Programme (agreement No. POIR.01.02.00-00-0352/16-00).

Figure 1. OneMeter beacon with optical sensor attached to IEC 62056-21 port of electricity meter.

II. SMART METERING CHALLENGES

A. *Smart Metering in Europe*

According to the data of the European Commission [4] and European energy regulators [5], so far only three EU members have achieved a full roll-out of smart meters: Italy, Finland, and Sweden. In 2015, in Denmark, Estonia, Malta, Slovenia, and Spain about half of the customers had had smart meters installed in their households, while in the Netherlands it was below 30%. In Austria, Latvia, Poland, and the UK, the household penetration was only about 10% (for Latvia) or below. In the rest of the EU countries, the deployment of smart meters had hardly started.

This means, for example, in Poland, where there are 8 million metering points, only less than 700 thousand are equipped with smart meters. However, a remarkable part of the remaining electricity meters are equipped with optical ports, which are normally used for billing readouts but can be equally used to access the meter readouts using an optical sensor.

B. *Existing Solutions*

Several solutions exist that aim to acquire energy consumption data from existing electronic, non-smart meters. The Rhino Company offers the so-called RhinoAMI AP device [6], which accesses electronic meters via a DIN bus using a cable

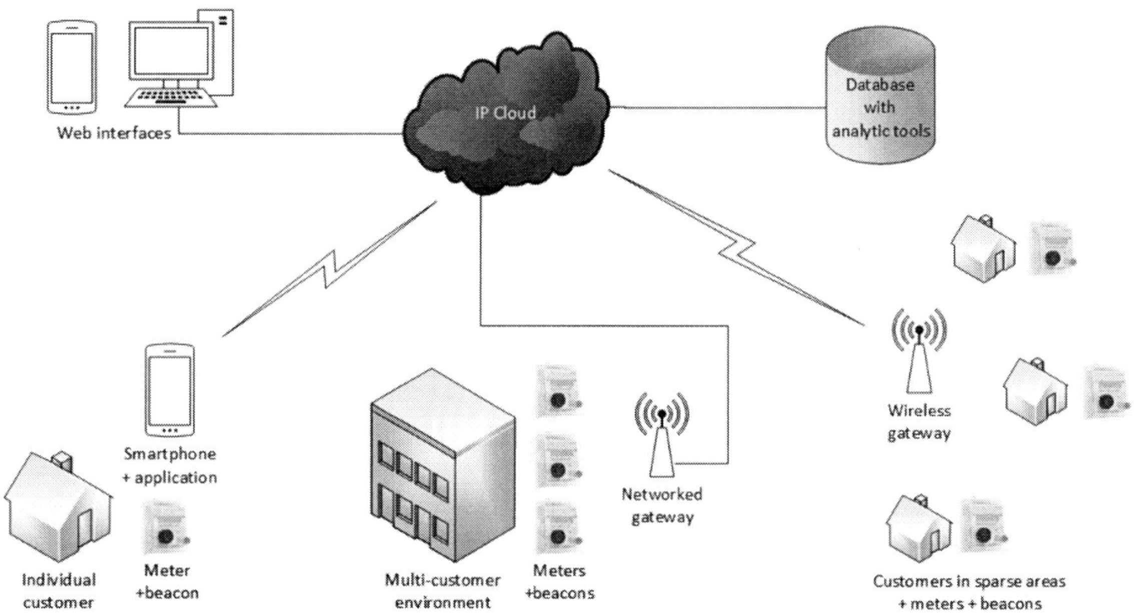

Figure 2. Schematic diagram of proposed OneMeter 2.0 system based on beacons with optical sensors.

connection. Metering data can be then transmitted further, using a GPRS or Ethernet connection. The device requires an external 5-12 V power source.

Smappee [7] is another cable solution, offered currently at 229 EUR, which, in contrast to the previously described system, uses an electromagnetic sensor clipped to the phase cable supplying an electrical installation, e.g., in an apartment or an office. A dedicated application allows the monitoring of the current energy consumption. A proprietary Non-Intrusive Load Monitoring (NILM) algorithm helps to recognize individual electrical appliances. The Smappee metering system is powered by a 100-230 V main supply. It is noteworthy that Smappee, in fact, estimates the consumption instead of reading it from the meter.

A device called mReader®Opto, produced by NUMERON [8], uses an optical sensor to communicate with the meter over the IEC 62056-21 protocol. It requires a USB connection to connect with a smartphone or a computer. It can work on a battery, but only for ca. 2h. The same producer also offers a gateway called smartBOX, which allows a remote transmission of the meter readouts over a network or GPRS.

REDZ Smart Communication Technologies offers another device with an optical sensor: KMK 118 Bluetooth Optical Probe [9]. Its functionality is similar to the previously described device, but here the cable communication is replaced by a wireless one. The device can be battery powered, but the battery life is reported to be only "greater than 24h". The device is offered at the price of 180 EUR.

C. *OneMeter 2.0 Project*

We are working on a system that utilizes beacons with optical sensors to read data directly from electricity meters. In contrast to other existing solutions, our beacons are energy efficient, allowing them to work on a single battery for over a year. Thanks to a cloud-based data platform and the use of smartphones, our solution enables a fast and cheap deployment of the AMI infrastructure using the existing, non-smart electricity meters.

III. Idea of Proposed Solution

The idea of our solution is based on using a small, energy-efficient wireless beacon with optical sensors attached to an electricity meter (see Figure 1). We propose employing either smartphones or dedicated gateways to transfer measurement data to the cloud, as shown schematically in Figure 2. The details of the proposed solution are described below.

A. *Optical Sensor in Beacon*

A small bottle cap-shaped beacon of 32 mm diameter (compatible with the IEC 62056-21 standard) was designed, equipped with an optical sensor, LED diode, Nordic Semiconductor's processor nRF51, flash memory, Bluetooth Low Energy (BLE) radio components, and a 3.0V battery (CR2032). The beacon is attached magnetically to an electronic meter equipped with an optical port. The optical sensor is designed with a miniature silicon photodiode of high radiant sensitivity and a low power comparator. The optical sensor, together with the IR LED diode, are able to set up communication with a meter using the IEC 62056-21 (old: IEC 1107) protocol. The amount of measurement data acquired from the meter depends on the meter's model – some of the meters present only the absolute active energy, while the others allow the readout of more detailed information, such as positive and negative active energy, or reactive energy.

The processor was programmed in such a way that the beacon performs a readout of the meter every 15 min and stores the metering data in the flash memory. The BLE component allows other BLE devices to connect to the beacon to download metering data or to transmit the readout in real time.

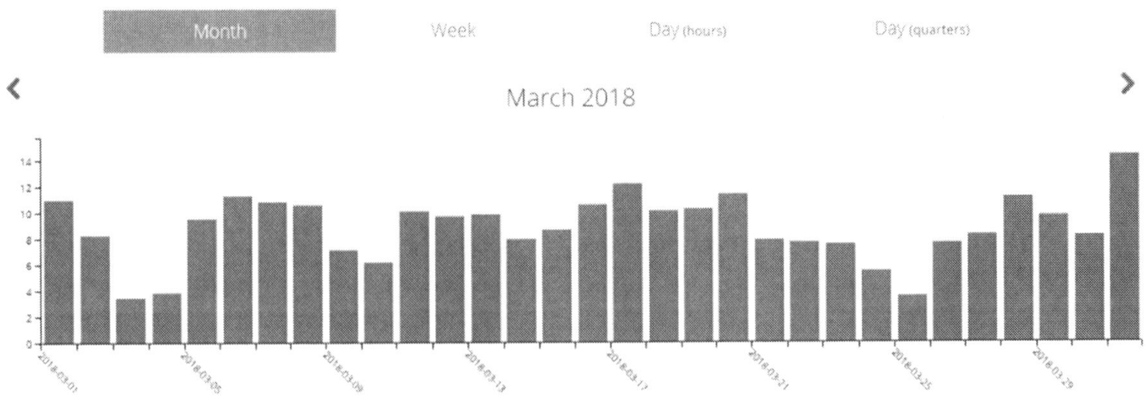

Figure 3. Sample monthly consumption chart for residential consumer. Values shown in [kWh].

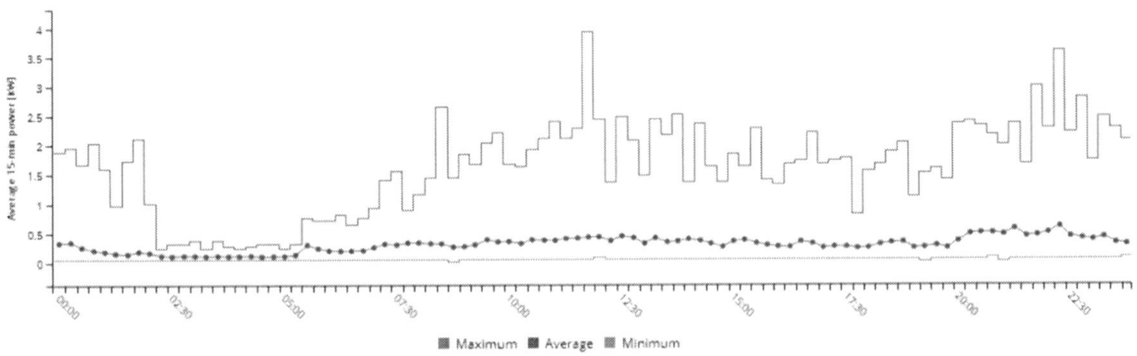

Figure 4. 15-minute daily consumption profile calculated over 2-month period for residential consumer.

B. *Smartphone as Gateway*

We decided to use smartphones as gateways to transmit measurement data from beacons to the cloud. We designed an Android application, which allows the setting up of data connections between the smartphone and the beacon. The connection is carried out using the BLE protocol version 4.0. When the connection is established, the measurement data, encrypted using the AES protocol, is sent to the data cloud over the smartphone's Internet connection, i.e., via Wi-Fi network or via a data connection from the mobile provider. The synchronization can be triggered by a user in arbitrary moments. The application can also operate in the gateway mode: in this case, the smartphone receives advertising packets and transfers them to the cloud.

Apart from using smartphones, we also plan to deploy dedicated gateways, which would communicate with the cloud using any of the IoT communication protocols, similarly to [10]. This option may be especially needed in rural areas, with less developed infrastructure, as depicted in Figure 2.

C. *Data Platform*

The data platform provides gathering, analysis, and visualizations of the collected metering data. The initial version of the platform was realized using the MongoDB database with a set of proprietary analytic algorithms.

A web-based user interface allows the visualization of the energy consumption data. The user is able to enter information about their tariff. Thanks to the tariff data imported to the database for various energy re-sellers, the cost estimation of the consumed energy can be calculated. The platform provides tools to generate reports showing consumption profiles for chosen date ranges and information about maximum power demand including, for example, information on the percentage of time a certain power threshold was exceeded.

IV. On-going Research Work

Intensive work on the OneMeter 2.0 system started at the beginning of 2018. The project highlights are presented below.

A. *Experimental Installations*

To verify experimentally how the solution works in a real environment, we needed to deploy it at the end users' locations. Up to the time of writing this article (October 2018) we have achieved the following approximate metrics:

- 160 business client installations (small and medium entrepreneurships);
- 20 household client installations;
- 40 installations in laboratory conditions;
- 76 meter models verified to work correctly with elaborated beacon;
- 0.8 million valid measurement records gathered in database starting from 1 Jan 2018.

In general, the experience built upon the above-described installations was very positive. Nevertheless, several issues were identified, which were then subject to improvements. One such issue was the problem introduced by Doze and App Standby feature in API level 23 (Android 6.0) – a power saving mechanism, which caused the gateway service installed on a smartphone to stop at random moments. This was solved by implementing the so-called wake lock feature, which prevents moving the gateway application into sleep mode by the smartphone's operating system.

B. *Energy Effectiveness of Beacon*

We performed several measurements to estimate the potential lifetime of the beacon with a single CR2032 battery. We took the following presumptions:

- 160 mAh of effective CR2032 battery capacity;
- 96 meter readouts per day (i.e., every 15 min);
- 650 B of data returned by the meter at 9600 baud rate;
- data collected by the gateway in real-time;
- 4 s BLE advertising interval.

Detailed information about the current demand and consequent battery usage by various beacon activities is shown in Table I.

TABLE I. BEACON ACTIVITIES WITHIN 15 MIN. WORK CYCLE.

Beacon activity	Current [μA]	Duration [s]	Time share [%]	Energy usage [μAh]	Energy share [%]
Meter readouts	978.04	3.46	0.38	0.94	21.95
BLE comm.	6038.71	1.24	0.14	2.08	48.78
Flash operations	3150.03	0.24	0.03	0.21	4.88
Idle	4.18	895.06	99.45	1.04	24.39

Energy consumption of ca. 4.27 μAh per 15 min. means that the daily beacon's energy consumption is on the level of 0.41 mAh. This implies that the beacon is now able to work without a battery replacement for about one year.

Based on [11] we estimated the foreseen energy consumption after adding support for a LPWAN network. For instance, assuming a LoRa with the lowest bitrate (250 b/s) the device would need a battery with at least 500 mAh capacity to send the daily single OBIS code data once per day. This requires replacing the CR2032 battery with AAA batteries to maintain at least one year of the beacon's uninterrupted operation.

C. *Initial Data Analysis and Visualization*

So far the data analytic platform allows users to access the following information:

- Monthly, weekly, daily, and 15-min. daily metrics of energy consumption (see Figure 3 for an example).
- 15-min daily consumption profile over an arbitrary period of time, showing average, minimum, and maximum consumption for every quarter (see Figure 4 for an example of a profile for a residential consumer calculated over two months).
- Information on the amount of the energy consumed during peak hours, off-peak hours, and during weekends.
- Cost of the consumed energy over the selected period for the selected tariff, showing the cost of electricity and distribution.
- Load duration curve, showing, e.g., the percentage of time when the power limit is exceeded.
- Comparison of hourly consumption profiles.

The initial feedback from the users, gathered using questionnaires, revealed that the clients were in general satisfied with the information available in the platform and the way it was visualized. However, the need for additional features (e.g., alerts) was reported and will be addressed soon in the project.

V. CONCLUSION AND FUTURE WORK

In this paper, we showed the on-going work on the OneMeter 2.0 system, which, thanks to the beacons with optical sensors, would be able to enhance the existing AMR electricity meters with smart functionality. Contrary to the solutions offered by the competitors, the described system is both wireless and energy-efficient. What is more, the cost of a single beacon is not likely to exceed several EUR, which is significantly lower than that for similar products available on the market.

The proposed system can be highly useful to end users, re-sellers, and distribution system operators (DSOs). Last but not least, the system may provide valuable information to prosumers, which would be able to monitor in real-time how much energy they both consume and produce.

The future work will involve intensive work on developing stand-alone gateways, including the ones using IoT communication protocols. Further work on increasing the beacon's energy efficiency is also foreseen.

REFERENCES

[1] European Union, "Directive 2012/27/EU of the European Parliament and of the COUNCIL of 25 October 2012 on energy efficiency, amending Directives 2009/125/EC and 2010/30/EU and repealing Directives 2004/8/EC and 2006/32/EC," Official Journal of the European Union, Nov. 2012.

[2] R. Morello, C. D. Capua, G. Fulco, and S. C. Mukhopadhyay, "A Smart Power Meter to Monitor Energy Flow in Smart Grids: The Role of Advanced Sensing and IoT in the Electric Grid of the Future," IEEE Sensors Journal, vol. 17, no. 23, Dec 2017, pp. 7828–7837.

[3] F. D. Garcia, F. P. Marafao, W. A. de Souza, and L. C. P. da Silva, "Power Metering: History and Future Trends," in 9th IEEE Green Technologies Conference (GreenTech 2017), March 2017, pp. 26–33.

[4] European Commission, "Second Report on the State of the Energy Union. Monitoring progress towards the Energy Union objectives – key indicators," Feb 2017.

[5] Agency for the Cooperation of Energy Regulators (ACER) and the Council of European Energy Regulators (CEER), "ACER/CEER Annual Report on the Results of Monitoring the Internal Electricity and Gas Markets in 2015 – Key Insights and Recommendations," Nov 2016.

[6] "Rhino Energy - Solution - Hardware," https://rhino.energy/hardware/, 2018, accessed 08 Jan 2019.

[7] "Smappee Energy," https://www.smappee.com/be_en/energy-monitor, 2018, accessed 08 Jan 2019.

[8] NUMERON, "Dokumentacja NUMERON, mReader®4," https://docs.numeron.pl/mreader4/, 2018, accessed 08 Jan 2019.

[9] REDZ Smart Communication Technologies Ltd., "KMK 119 – Bluetooth optical probe - Smart wireless auto protocols detection probe," http://probeformeters.com/brochure/REDZ_KMK119_Detailed_Datasheet.pdf, 2018, accessed 08 Jan 2019.

[10] M. Carratú, M. Ferro, A. Pietrosanto, and V. Paciello, "Smart Power Meter for the IoT," in IEEE 16th International Conference on Industrial Informatics (INDIN 2018), July 2018, pp. 514–519.

[11] E. Morin, M. Maman, R. Guizzetti, and A. Duda, "Comparison of the Device Lifetime in Wireless Networks for the Internet of Things," IEEE Access, vol. 5, 2017, pp. 7097–7114.

Research for Improvement of Resolution of Distance Sensor Using Fluctuation of Laser Terminal Voltage due to Self Coupling Effect

Tatsuya Ohba, Norio Tsuda, Jun Yamada
Dept. of Electrical and Electronics Engineering
Aichi Institute of Technology, AIT
Toyota, Japan
E-mail: v18706vv@aitech.ac.jp

Abstract— **When acquire signal due to the self-coupling effect from the terminal voltage of the laser, the signal-to-noise ratio gets worse. Because it is difficult to detect the signal, so it was impossible to measure the distance with a resolution of 1 cm or less. In this study, we proposed a new noise reduction method, that could carry out measurement for a resolution of 1 cm or less, which has not been done before. From the experimental results, we reported the factors that cause the errors in the distance sensor employing a self-coupling effect.**

Keywords-Self coupling effect; distance sensor; terminal voltage; Vertical Cavity Surface Emitting LASER.

I. INTRODUCTION

Generally, the light intensity of a Laser Diode (LD) slightly fluctuates when part of the light scattered on the target surface interferes with the laser light on its active layer. Self-coupled laser sensors make use of this variation for distance [1], [2], micro displacement [3], [4], velocity measurement [5], [6] and so on. Aside from fluctuations of light intensity, self-coupling effect also causes fluctuations of the terminal voltage [7], which can be used, instead of the photodiode (PD), to develop a compact and inexpensive photodetector free sensor can be realized. Conventional, researches on laser distance sensors utilizing laser terminal voltage fluctuations caused by self-coupling effect, found out their wide range of applications, such as for position control of robot arms, collision avoidance, shape measurement, etc.

A self-coupled laser distance sensor detects a signal called Mode Hop Pulse (MHP). The MHP changes proportionally with distance, and this property allows distance measurement to be done. MHP will be explained fully in section II.

The theoretical resolution of distance measuring equipment using MHP is determined by laser and circuit characteristics; in current researches, this is 0.44 mm, allowing a measurement accuracy at intervals of only 1cm. In this paper, we measured the accuracy at an interval of less than 1 cm. The measurement principle is shown in Section III, and the measurement results are shown in Section IV. The conclusion is described in section V.

II. DISTANCE MEASUREMENT PRINCIPLE

In this section, we will briefly summarize the principles of the self-coupling effect, as it has been fully explained in the previous studies [8]. In the same longitudinal mode, the oscillation wavelength of a LD varies proportionally with the applied voltage. Moreover, when half the wavelength and the set of integer n are equal to the measurement distance, the fluctuation of the applied voltage due to the self-coupling effect is maximized. If a triangular wave modulation is applied to the LD, then a periodic fluctuation occurs, as shown in Figure 1. From the same figure, the dotted line shows the applied triangular wave voltage waveform, while the solid line indicates the resonance condition satisfied at equal intervals, thus, resulting to a step wise pulse that is superimposed on the applied voltage. The periodic voltage fluctuation due to the self-coupling effect is called MHP.

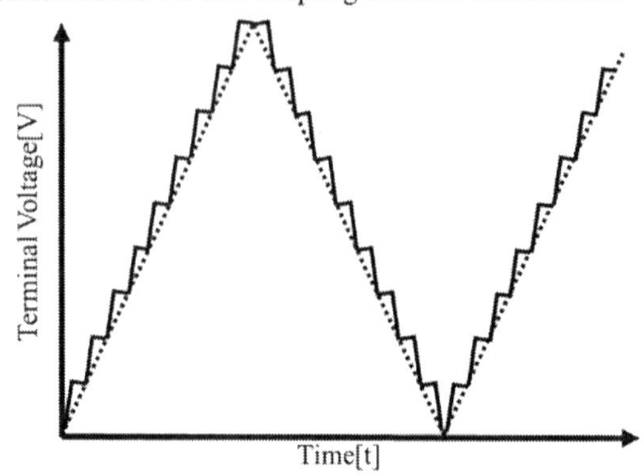

Figure 1. Schematic of the MHP.

The average frequency of all MHPs generated during one period of the modulated signal varies in proportion with the distance. Moreover, their frequencies are all equal when the total speed difference between the sensor and the object (Figure 1). The distance resolution of the self-coupled laser distance sensor is the length that the MHP changes by one, and the measurable distance is determined by the coherence length of the LD. Conventionally, the fast Fourier transform (FFT) is used to acquire the MHP frequency output of considerable white Gaussian noise (WGN), from the laser terminal voltage.

III. MEASUREMENT SYSTEM

Figure 2 shows a schematic of the distance measurement system.

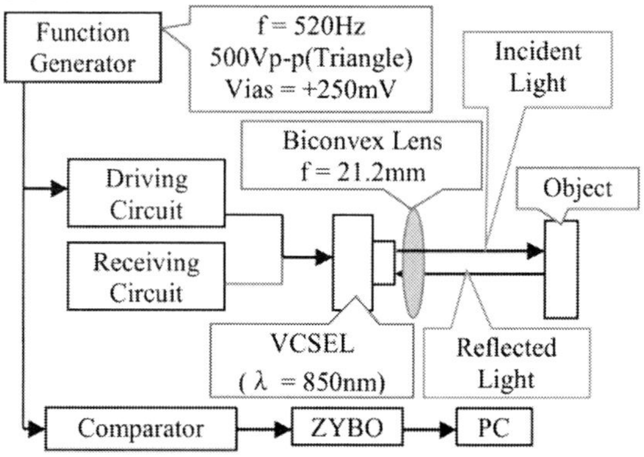

Figure. 2 Block diagram of distance measurement system.

The Vertical Cavity Surface Emitting LASER (VCSEL) is a ULM850-B2-PL-S46FZP (ULM850), having a 850 nm wavelength, a 2 mW light intensity output, a single beam mode, and a circular polarization. The laser driver applies a 520 Hz triangular wave with a 1.8 mA p-p triangular current. The ULM850 modulation efficiency is 0.46 nm/mA. The receiver is designed as a multistage band pass filter (BPF) with 2500 times amplification, and upper and lower cut-off frequency limits of 2 MHz and 100 kHz, respectively. The laser beam is adjusted to yield a collimated beam and the target object is a white paper. The comparator digitalizes the laser terminal voltage because the system-on-chip (SoC) device used only supports digital signals.

The MHP frequency is measured using an SoC device named ZYBO. In the FFT using ZYBO, the sampling frequency is 3.2 MHz, four FFT processed spectral data were averaged to reduce noise.

IV. MEASUREMENT RESULT

Figure 3 shows the results of the distance measurement. Because the resolution of the time FFT is about 1.5 mm, the measurement interval was set to 3 mm.

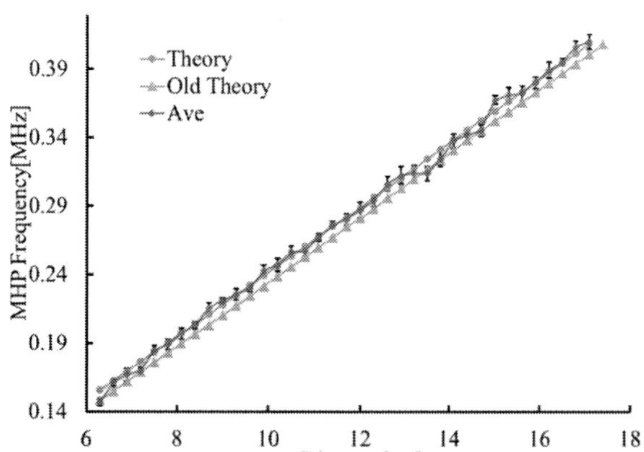

Figure.3. Result of distance measurement.

The measurement distance was in the range 6.3 to 16.4 cm. Ave is an experimental value obtained by averaging the results obtained from repeating the measurements 20 times in each distance. The optical path length becomes longer than the actual due to the refractive index of the lens. The theoretical value corrected by considering the influence of the lens is Theory, and the theoretical value not considered is Old Theory. From the comparison of the respective data, the theoretical values before correction did not match with the experimental values; however, the corrected theoretical values agreed with the experimental values.

V. CONCLUSION

When the laser output light interferes with the returning light, the terminal voltage of LD slightly fluctuates. On the other hand, when the triangular wave modulation is applied to the applied voltage, the voltage frequency fluctuates due to the self-coupling effect generated during one cycle of the modulation signal, which varies in proportion to the distance. Therefore, by measuring the distance signal (MHP) from the fluctuation of the terminal voltage of the LD, the distance can be measured without PD. The measurement conducted for this study was for a resolution of 1 cm or less, which has not been verified so far. The results revealed that it is necessary to measure by taking into consideration the influence of the refractive index of the lens in the measurement of 1 cm or less.

REFERENCES

[1] Yah Leng Lim, K.Bertling, et.al,"Displacement and distance measurement using the change in junction voltage across a laser diode due to the self-mixing effect", Proc.SPIE Vol.6038 60381O (2006).

[2] Gregory Mourat, Noel Servagent,Thierry M.Bosch,"Distance measurement using the self-mixing efect in a three-electrode distributed Bragg reflector laser diode", Opt. Eng. 39(03), pp.738-743 (2000).

[3] T. Gharbi, A. Courtevill and A. Chebbour,"Backscatter-modulated laser diode for low-frequency small-amplitude vibration measurement", Appl. Opt. 36, pp.8233-8237 (1997).

[4] G. Giuliani, S. Donati, and L. Monti,"Self-mixing laser diode vibrometer with wide dynamic range", Proc. SPIE Vol. 4827, pp.353-362 (2002)

[5] P. J. Groot, G. M. Gallatin, and S. H. Macomber,"Ranging and velocimetry signal generation in a backscatter-modulated laser diode", Appl. Opt. 21, No. 21, pp.4475-4480 (1988)

[6] L. Krehut, J. Hast, E. Alarousu, and R. Myllyla,"Low cost velocity sensor based on the self-mixing effect in a laser diode", Opto-Electronics Rev. 11, No. 4, pp.313-319 (2003)

[7] J. Hashizume, S. Shinada, F. Koyama, K. Iga,"Reflection Induced Voltage Change of Surface Emitting Laser for Optical Probing", Opt. Rev. 9 p. 186 (2002)

[8] Takeshi Yoshimatsu, Norio Tsuda, Jun Yamada,"Signal Processing for Distance Measurement Using Laser Voltage Fluction Due to Self-Coupling Effect", SandM, Vol.29,No. 9 pp.1315-1324 (2017)

Frequency and Intensity Decision of Laser Microphone using Deep Leaning

Ryota Mori, Norio Tsuda, Jun Yamada
Dept. of Electrical and Electronics Engineering
Aichi Institute of Technology, AIT
Toyota, Japan
E-mail: v18723vv@aitech.ac.jp

Abstract—**Laser Microphones do not use a diaphragm, and are hence able to detect sound waves over a wide frequency band, from low frequency waves to ultrasonic waves. They can also measure sound waves in fluids, such as under water, without contact. However, the output signal of the Laser Microphone has many superimposed noise components, digital filter processing may be necessary and there was a disadvantage that the amount of processing increased. Therefore, we verified whether the desired frequency and sound pressure intensity can be determined even in the presence of superimposed noise by learning the output signal in the non-processed state via Deep Learning. As a result, when the number of epochs corresponding to the learning amount is 500, frequency judgment was generally possible.**

Keywords-: Laser Microphone; self-coupling effect; deep learning;

I. INTRODUCTION

These days, many researches are actively and extensively engaged on the development of optical microphones that do not use a diaphragm, yet could detect sound waves over a wide band range, in fluid, and the like. Laser Microphone, which applies a self-coupling effect of a semiconductor Laser Diode (LD), has broadband and flat frequency characteristics, and is capable of 360° omnidirectional audio detection on a plane perpendicular to the laser optical axis [1]. However, many noise components are superimposed on the output signal of the Laser Microphone. Thus, after performing fast Fourier transform (FFT), it is necessary to judge its frequency and sound pressure intensity by carrying out digital processing.

However, there was a disadvantage that the amount of processing increased. Therefore, we verified by learning the output signal in the non-processed state via Deep Learning, whether the desired frequency and intensity can be determined even in the presence of superimposed noise. Moreover, it could be assumed that a state where it is impossible to judge the threshold by superimposing many noises could be avoided. This paper is organized as follows. Section II describes the principle and system of measurement using Deep Learning, Section III describes the measurement results, and Section IV summarizes what were found from the measurement results.

II. MEASUREMENT PRINCIPLE AND SYSTEM

The Sound wave detection in laser optical employs the self-coupling effect of LD. The self-coupling effect is a phenomenon in which the optical output of the LD slightly increases and decreases by returning a part of the laser optical emitted from the LD into the active layer by the reflecting material. Figure 1 shows the operating principle of the Laser Microphone.

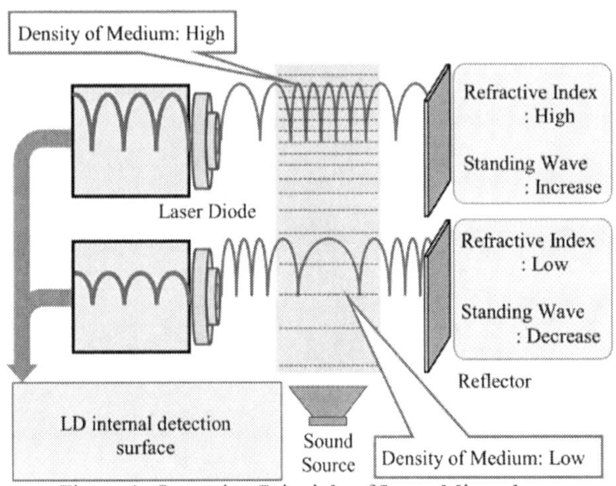

Figure 1. Operating Principle of Laser Microphone

Because sound waves are longitudinal waves, the density of the medium changes. High medium density increases slightly the refractive index of optical. On the contrary, low medium density also decreases the refractive index of optical. By repeating their states, the phase of the standing wave of the optical interference generated by the self-coupling effect periodically changes. The phase change of the optical interference coincides with the incident sound wave, and the change amount is proportional to the intensity. Thus, the frequency and intensity can be measured in the same way as a typical microphone.

The measurement system of frequency and intensity decision using Deep Learning is shown in Figure 2. LD uses a Distributed Feedback Laser diode (DFB-Laser), and the optical output was continuously oscillated at 25 mW. The prism sheet was used as the reflection plate was set to 10 cm.

A sound source was installed in a place 20 cm away so as to go straight to the laser beam. These measurement systems were fixed inside the anechoic box by a magnet. The output signal is processed by the personal computer. The Operating System (OS) of the personal computer uses Ubuntu16.04, while the framework for Deep Learning uses Chainer.

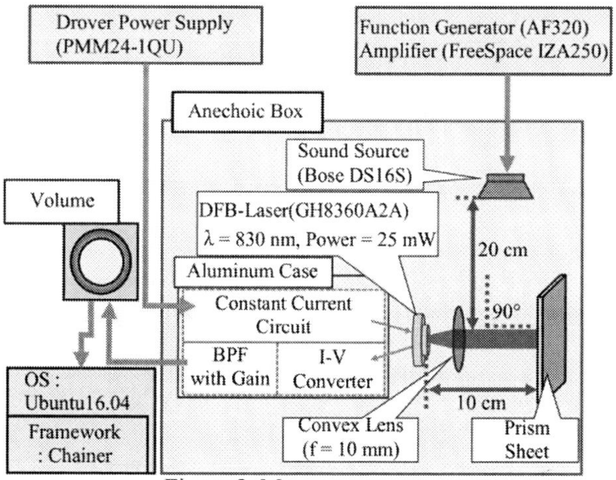

Figure 2. Measurement system

An overview of the Deep Learning program is shown in Figure 3. Neural network uses Recurrent Neural Network (RNN) with return value in the Hidden layer.

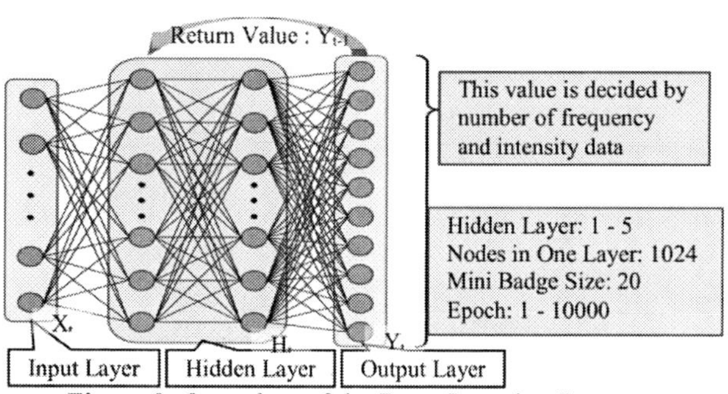

Figure 3. Overview of the Deep Learning Program

The number of nodes for one layer was 1024 and the mini batch size was fixed to 20, the number of epochs corresponding to the learning amount, and hidden layers are varied, and the frequency and intensity decision were carried out to measure the loss.

III. Measurement Results

In this abstract, the result is shown in Figure 4 when 100 Hz to 1 kHz sound waves are indent every 100 Hz and number of epoch is changed. The result of a typical microphone for comparison with the Laser Microphone is also shown in Figure 4.

In the same figure, the loss of decision using the Laser Microphone decreased until the number of epoch reached 500. This was because the output signal of the Laser Microphone contained a lot of noise components, error propagation within the program did not work well, and over-learning may have occurred.

On the other hand, when measuring with typical microphone, the losses decrease just like in the Laser Microphone. However, over-learning did not occur and the losses were approaching zero at an epoch of 500 or greater.

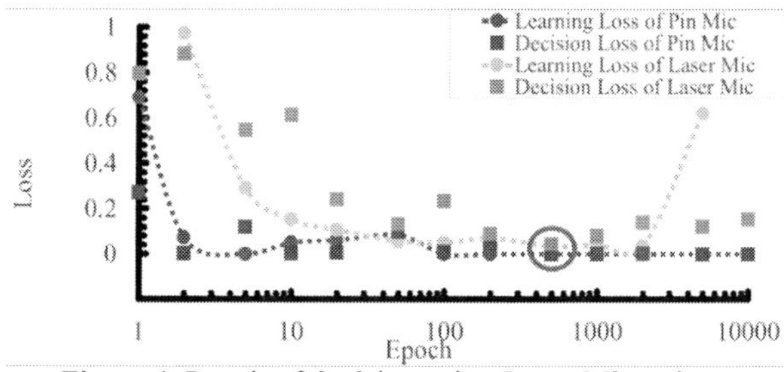

Figure 4. Result of decision using Laser Microphone

Moreover, the loss in both cases is smallest at an epoch of 500. Therefore, Epoch = 500 was assumed as the optimum place and the reference point where the Deep Learning program was created.

Figure 5 shows the answer rate for each frequency due to the change in epoch.

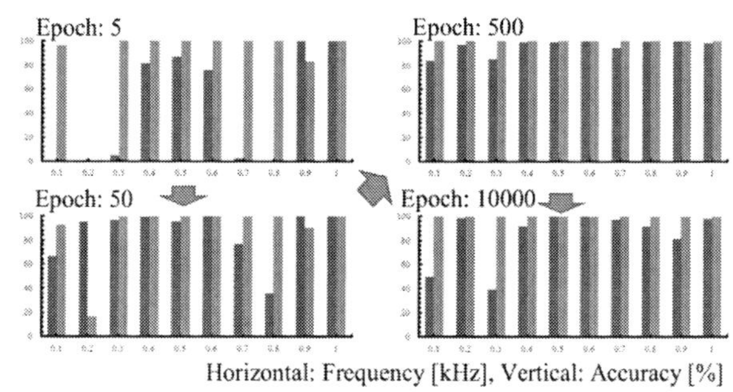

Figure 5. Result of decision using typical microphone

From Figure 5, in case of misjudgment, the desired frequency was judged as "Frequency of Adjacent".

IV. Conclusion

We found that it is possible to judge the frequency of the Laser Microphone using Deep Learning. Moreover, the Deep Learning program experiences the smallest loss when the number of epoch is 500. Future research will deal with the increase in the number of learning data and whether Laser Microphone can be used as a sound level meter for digital display. Furthermore, the results of change in loss due to change in hidden layers and intensity decision will be announced on the day of the conference.

References

[1] D. Mizushima, T. Yoshimatsu, K. Goshima, N. Tsuda, and J. Yamada: "SoundDetection by Laser Microphone Using Self-coupling of Semiconductor Laser" IEEJ Trans. EIS, Vol. 136-C, No. 7, pp. 1021-1026, 2016.

Prediction of Resident's Outing Time for Energy Saving

Sanghun Kim
Energy IT Convergence Research Center, Convergence System R&D Division, Korea Electronics Technology Institute, Republic of Korea.
ksh7150@keti.re.kr

Jungmee Yun
Energy IT Convergence Research Center, Convergence System R&D Division, Korea Electronics Technology Institute, Republic of Korea.
yunjm@keti.re.kr

Kiwoong Kwon
Energy IT Convergence Research Center, Convergence System R&D Division, Korea Electronics Technology Institute, Republic of Korea.
kiwoong.kwon@keti.re.kr

Sanghak Lee
Energy IT Convergence Research Center, Convergence System R&D Division, Korea Electronics Technology Institute, Republic of Korea.
sanghaklee88@keti.re.kr

***Abstract*—By analyzing the occupancy pattern of the user, it is possible to find out the time when they are expected to go out. Based on this, if Heating, Ventilation, and Air Conditioning (HVAC) can be controlled in advance, energy consumption can be reduced. The buildings are basically equipped with insulation technology, so they can maintain indoor comfort for a certain period of time even after ceasing HVAC system. Therefore, by predicting the time when the user goes out and performing the pre-control of the HVAC, the energy-saving effect can be obtained. In this paper, we propose a technique to detect periodic and repetitive outing of the resident by analyzing user's occupancy pattern. By pre-control of the HVAC with occupancy, the energy consumption can be reduced without harming the comfort of the user.**

Keywords- Occupancy Sensor; Occupancy Probability; Energy Saving; HVAC.

I. Introduction

Reducing energy use is a very important issue in terms of economic, environmental and social aspects. Users can achieve economic benefits by reducing energy costs, and the government can realize social values by reducing the cost of constructing power plants and the cost of energy imports. This energy saving is very important because it can slow down climate change and protect the environment [1]. For this rea-son, various technologies have been developed as energy saving methods; however it is known that it is most important to reduce wasted energy.

Some researches on room temperature control based on occupancy probability have been carried out [2][3]. However, these researches focused on the comfort of the users and did not consider saving energy.

In this paper, we analyze user's repetition pattern (absence and presence) by energy conservation method and try to find out the time of going out. By using this point of departure, energy consumption can be reduced by shutting down or lowering the output of devices, such as Heating, Ventilation, and Air Conditioning (HVAC). Since the buildings are equipped with basic insulation technology, the comfort of the room is not significantly degraded even after the cooling / heating interruption. Therefore, when the user is expected to go out, even if the HVAC device is shut down earlier, the comfort of the user is not impaired and the energy consumption is expected to be reduced.

This paper is organized as follows. Section 2 describes the outing prediction process. Section 3 describes the brief results obtained from our experiment. Finally, Section IV presents our conclusions and future works.

II. Outing Prediction

The proposed method performs clustering based on user's occupancy data. This is because the user's repetition pattern changes depending on whether the day is working day or not. At this time, it is also possible to consider using calendar information, user schedule and location; however in this paper, only the occupancy sensor data is used. By using the information such as the planner and global positioning system (GPS) of the smartphone and Google calendar, it is possible to know the time when the user goes out. In this case, however, there are side effects such as a risk of personal information leakage and hardware unit price increase. Therefore, in this paper, we tried to predict user outage time by analyzing only occupancy data.

Since the calendar data is not used in this study, data for each date are assigned to 7 groups in order (using the repetition of seven days in a week), and finally divided into two clusters using *K*-means clustering algorithm [4] (holidays and working days). For each of these two clusters, the non-parametric estimation technique kernel density estimation (KDE) [5] with Epanechnikov kernel is used [6]. Through the process, the discrete-time probability is converted into continuous-time probability and smoothing effects can also be expected.

III. Results

In order to evaluate the performance of the proposed technique, Passive Infra-Red (PIR) sensor is used. Data received from the sensors were divided into 30 minute intervals, and the decision whether the user is occupied or not was made.

In this paper, we use three experimental rooms to obtain the resident's occupancy information and to derive the probabilities. The list of rooms used is shown in Table 1. Experimental occupancy data were obtained from August 1 to August 30, 2018 (this is the hottest season in Korea and has the most energy use). The clustering results were shown in Figure 1. Clustering results are the same in all three experimental rooms. Therefore, only one representative is shown. Data of working days were extracted from these two clusters. During the working days and holidays, we focused on working days (i.e., cluster 1 from Figure 1.). Figures 2 to 4 show the probability of occupancy. In these figures, it can be seen that the probability of dropping below 0.5 is the estimated time of going out. Therefore, energy savings can be achieved by turning off the HVAC systems before that point.

IV. Conclusions and Future Works

In this paper, we have performed outing time prediction based on the user's occupancy probability, and found that energy savings can be achieved by shutting down or lowering the output of HVAC equipment before the user's estimated time of departure.

The actual energy saving effect is under investigation, and we will find out by demonstration how much energy we can save. In addition, although this paper focuses on offices only, studies on general housing will be conducted. The authors are preparing a paper containing these new contents.

Acknowledgment

This work was supported by the Korea Institute of Energy Technology Evaluation and Planning (KETEP) and the Ministry of Trade, Industry & Energy (MOTIE) of the Republic of Korea (No. 20161210200670).

The authors would like to appreciate the anonymous reviewers, whose comments and suggestions improved the quality of this manuscript.

References

[1] E. A. Abdelaziz, R. Saidur, and S. Mekhilef, "A Review on Energy Saving Strategies in Industrial Sector," Renewable and Sustainable Energy Reviews, vol. 15, pp. 150-168, Jan. 2011.

[2] J. Scott, et. al., "PreHeat: Controlling Home Heating Using Occupancy Prediction," in Proc. ACM Int'l Conf. Ubiquitous Computing, pp. 281-290, Sep. 2011.

[3] C. Koehler, B. D. Ziebart, J. Mankoff, and A. K. Dey, " TherML: Occupancy Prediction for Thermostat Control," in Proc. ACM Int'l Conf. Ubiquitous Computing, pp. 103-112, Sep. 2013.

[4] C. M. Bishop, Pattern Recognition and Machine Learning. New York: Springer, 2006.

[5] J.-P. Vert, K. Tsuda, and V. Schölkopf, "A Primer on Kernel Methods," in Kernel Methods in Computational Biology, J.-P. Vert, K. Tsuda, V. Schölkopf Ed. MIT press 2004, pp. 35–70.

[6] A. K. Jain, R. P. W. Duin, and J. Mao, "Statistical Pattern Recognition: A Review," IEEE Trans. Pattern Analysis and Machine Intelligence, vol. 22, no. 1, pp. 4-37, Jan. 2000.

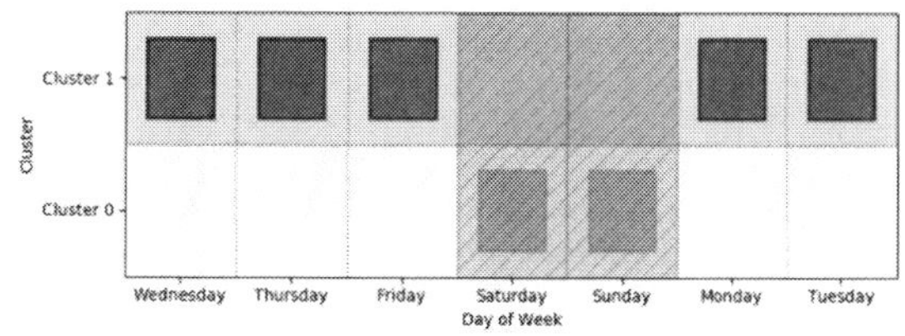

Figure 1. Clustering results of the occupancy data.

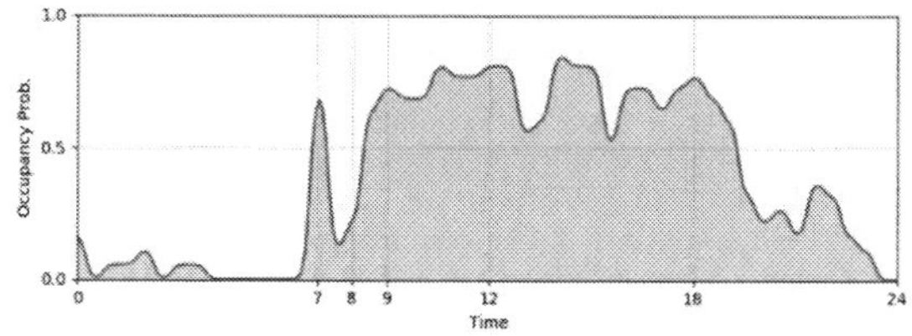

Figure 2. Occupancy probability of the first experimental room 1.

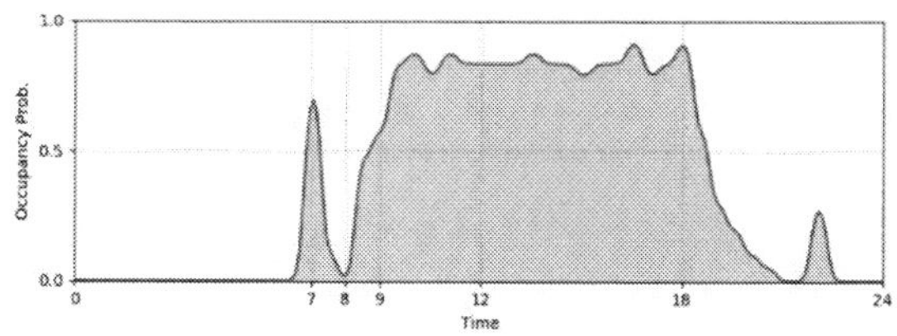

Figure 3. Occupancy probability of the second experimental room.

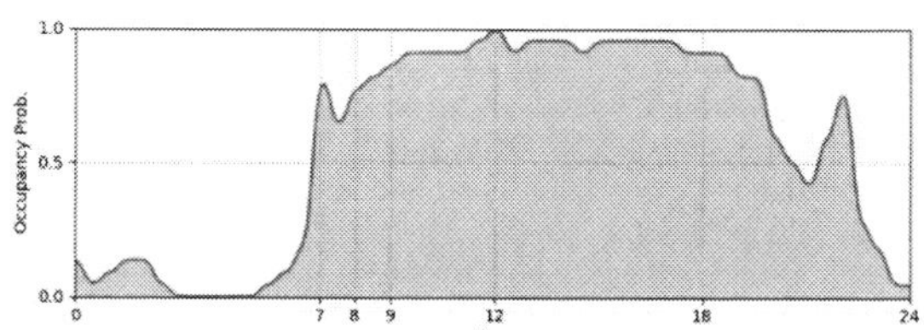

Figure 4. Occupancy probability of the third experimental room.

TABLE 1. LIST OF ROOMS FOR DATA ACQUISITION AND EXPERIMENT.

Place	Type	Area	Number of Usual Resident
Room 1	Office	57.36 m^2	4
Room 2	Office	60.66 m^2	7
Room 3	Office	79.34 m^2	4

Demand Response Enabled Artificial Intelligence based Air Conditioning System

Kiwoong Kwon, Sanghun Kim, Jungmee Yun, Byungmin Kim, and Sanghak Lee

Energy IT Convergence Research Center,
Korea Electronics Technology Institute, Korea
Email: {kiwoong.kwon, ksh7150, yunjm, 6954kbm, sanghaklee88}@keti.re.kr

Abstract—**Recently, as energy smart metering and remote control of smart devices become possible, Demand Response (DR) in home and small building is increasing. In this paper, we propose a DR enabled AI based air conditioning system to overcome the energy shortage problem in summer. It derives users' comfortable temperature by learning temperature and humidity, and automatically controls the air conditioner based on derived temperature. In addition, when DR is issued, the energy peak control based on the Predicted Mean Vote (PMV) is performed, thereby minimizing the user comfort degradation and finding DR resource. The experiment was conducted based on the test bed and we have shown its feasibility.**

Keywords–Demand Response; Artificial Intelligence; Predicted Mean Vote; Air Conditioning System

I. Introduction

Demand for energy continues to globally increase and a tremendous social expense is required to recover from the yearly arising blackouts. In recent years, there has been a growing concern about the energy shortage, as the energy consumption in summer and winter has increased sharply due to abnormal climates, such as heat and cold waves [1].

Demand Response (DR) refers to a technology that balances energy demand and supply by adjusting electricity rate and instructing load reduction when energy supply crisis arises. Previously, DR studies mainly carry out to prevent power outage in the factory or building. However, as remote control of various home appliances in the smart home has become possible thanks to the improvement of the Internet of Things technology, DR in home and small buildings is also being studied [2].

In this paper, we have proposed DR Enabled Artificial Intelligence based Air Conditioning System to overcome the energy shortage problem due to soaring energy use in the summer. The air conditioning system predicts the Predicted Mean Vote (PMV) [3] of each home using artificial intelligence technology and automatically controls the air conditioner based on the derived temperature by PMV. When DR signal is issued, the air conditioning system adjusts the temperature of each home according the learned PMV that reflects user's preferred comfort level. The experiment was conducted based on the test bed and we have shown its feasibility.

The rest of this paper is organized as follows. Section II describes the system design, and Section III evaluates the proposed system by conducting the experiment. Finally, we conclude this paper in Section IV.

II. Design of AI based Air Conditioning System

Figure 1 outlines the proposed AI-based Air Conditioning System. It is comprised of the air conditioner controller, the database server, and the learning and control system. The air conditioner controller plays a role in sending a control data by the remote controller and periodically measured environmental data (e.g., temperature, humidity, occupancy) to the database server. Since it is equipped with an IR transceiver, IR signal sniffed from the remote controller can be converted into a control message.

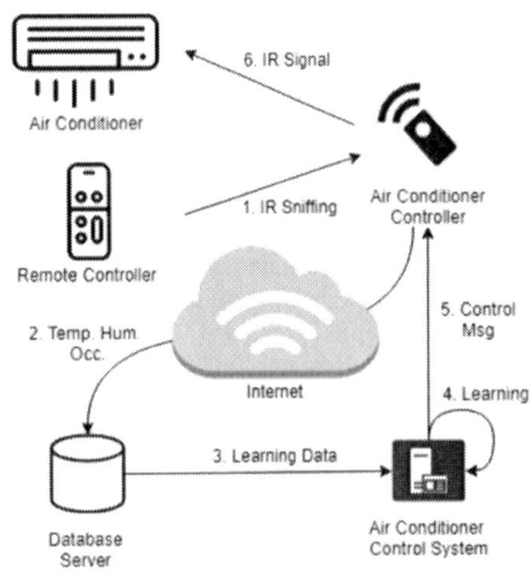

Figure 1. Overview of AI based Air Conditioning System

The database server plays a role in storing data sent from the air conditioner controller through RESTful web APIs. The data includes temperature, humidity, and occupancy. Occupancy data is expressed as 0 (unoccupied) or 1 (occupied) to determine if the user is occupying the home.

The learning and control system learns the temperature and humidity data obtained from the database server and generates PMV learning model using an artificial neural network. The temperature and humidity data is not used for learning when the occupancy data is 0, and PMV stands among the most recognized thermal comfort models that express satisfaction with the thermal environment.

After the PMV learning model is generated, it derives the current comfortable temperature of the home by assigning the current humidity as a parameter to the PMV learning model and sends the control message containing the derived temperature to the air conditioner controller every 10 minutes. The air conditioner controller generates IR signal corresponding to the received control message and controls the air conditioner.

The control mode is divided into comfort and economy

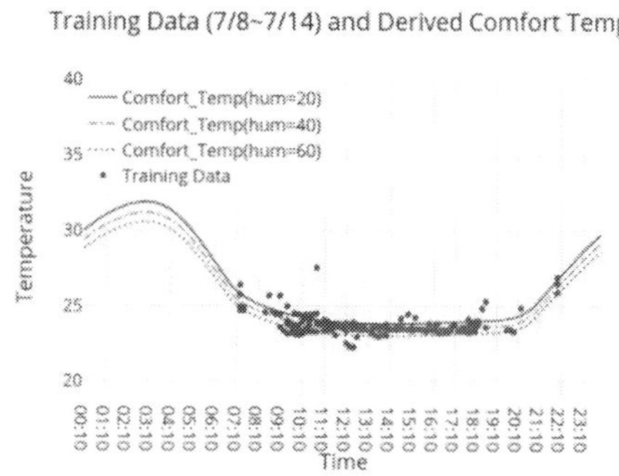

Figure 2. Training Data and Predicted Comfortable Temperature Graph based on PMV Learning Model

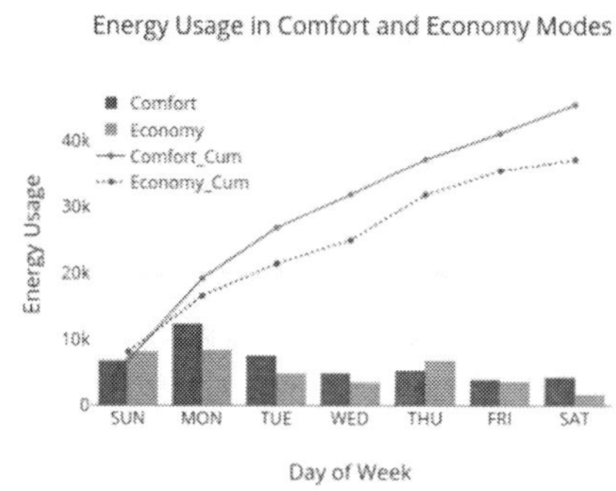

Figure 3. Comparison of Energy Usage in Comfort (7/15-7/21) and Economy (7/22-7/28) modes

modes which are set by users' smartphone. In the comfort mode, the air conditioner is controlled by the derived comfortable temperature, and in the economy mode, it is controlled to be 2 degrees higher. However, if the user changes the temperature while the air conditioner is operating automatically, the adjusted temperature is added to the previous training data for the next learning. This allows the user's intention to be continuously reflected in the training data, thereby improving the user's satisfaction.

When the DR signal is issued, the air conditioner control system queries the user through the smartphone whether to join the DR. For the users joining the DR, their air conditioner is controlled so as to minimize the difference between the adjustable PMV and the learned comfortable PMV to minimize the deterioration of the user comfort. This can be expressed by the following equation;

$$Minimize : \sum_{i=0}^{N-1} |PMV(i) - cPMV(i)| \quad (1)$$

where $PMV(i)$ is adjustable PMV of home i through temperature control when the DR signal is issued, $cPMV(i)$ is learned comfortable PMV of home i, and N is the number of houses participating in DR. According to the above equation, the air conditioner is initially controlled by assigning $cPMV(i)$ to $PMV(i)$ which minimizes $|PMV(i) - cPMV(i)|$. However, if the amount of energy saved is insufficient, $PMV(i)$ increases until it reaches the target energy savings. This minimizes the deterioration of comfort by DR.

III. Experiment and Evaluation

Experiments based on the test bed were carried out to verify the feasibility of the proposed AI based air conditioning system. The test bed was constructed at a room in Korea Electronics Technology Institute. We collected temperature, humidity, occupancy data of the room from July 8th to 14th, 2018 and generated the PMV learning model based on these data. Note that actual test bed will be extended in the future.

Figure 2 shows the training data of temperature for 7 days, and the predicted comfortable temperature graph derived from PMV learning model. The dots represent training data, and the solid, dashed-dotted, and dotted lines show a comfortable temperature graph in humidity 20, 40, 60, respectively. The learning data distribution and the derived comfortable temperature graph have a similar pattern, which shows that the derived comfortable temperature reflects the user's preference. Using this derived comfortable temperature while DR operates, the air conditioner is controlled according to the comfort level, minimizing the deterioration of comfort in the home and encouraging participation in the DR.

Figure 3 shows the energy usage difference between the comfort (7/15-7/21) and economy modes (7/22-28). The left and right bars on day of week show daily energy usage in the comfort and economy modes, and the solid and dotted lines show cumulative energy usage in the comfort and economy modes. The difference between cumulative energy usage in economy and comfort modes shows a tendency to increase with time. Comparing these on Saturday, the economy mode uses about 8.2 kW (= 45437-37168) less than the comfort mode. This represents the amount of electricity that can be saved by controlling the temperature, which can be used to determine the amount of temperature that needs to be adjusted to meet the target energy savings during DR operation.

IV. Conclusion and Future Work

In this paper, we have proposed the demand response enabled artificial intelligence based air conditioning system. The proposed system generates the PMV learning model by learning temperature and humidity data, and performs PMV based air conditioner control considering the user comfort level when the demand response signal is issued. Experiments were performed on a test bed and showed the feasibility of the proposed system. For future research, we will apply current work to the large scaled test bed and measure the performance.

Acknowledgment

This work was supported by the Korea Institute of Energy Technology Evaluation and Planning(KETEP) and the Ministry of Trade, Industry & Energy(MOTIE) of the Republic of Korea (No. 20161210200670).

References

[1] C. A. Craig and S. Feng, "Exploring utility organization electricity generation, residential electricity consumption, and energy efficiency: A climatic approach," Applied Energy, vol. 185, no. N/A, pp. 779–790, 2017.

[2] H.Park, H. Park, S. Lee, and J. Choi, "Design Analysis of Multicast Based Lightweight Demand Response Protocol for Energy IoT Environment," J. KICS, vol. 43, no. 7, pp. 1163–1175, 2018.

[3] P. O. Fanger, "Thermal comport. Analysis and applications in environmental engineering," Copenhagen: Danish Technical Press, 2018.

A Study on Prediction Model of Energy Consumption for Demand Response Service of Wastewater Treatment Facility

Byungmin Kim, Eunggi Lee, Kiwoong Kwon, Jungmee Yun
Energy IT Convergence Research Center
Korea Electronics Technology Institute, Republic of Korea
E-mail: {6954kbm, leg429, kiwoong.kwon, yunjm}@keti.re.kr

***Abstract*—Recently, high-power-demanding wastewater treatment processes have been introduced in the wastewater treatment facilities according to the strict water quality standard of the effluent water. The influent water quality of the wastewater treatment facilities differs according to environmental factors. However, the processes of the wastewater treatment facilities are operated with the maximum load to meet the effluent water quality standard. The wastewater treatment facilities can be utilized as a demand response resource by analyzing the wastewater treatment process and power usage patterns according to the influent water quality. In this study, we describe the power measurement system, the power usage pattern, and the power consumption prediction model of the wastewater treatment facility for the application of demand response service.**

Keywords-Demand Response; Energy Consumption Prediction; Neural Network; Power Measurement System; Wastewater Treatment Facility

I. INTRODUCTION

High-power-demanding wastewater treatment processes have been introduced in the wastewater treatment facilities. As of 2015, the electricity consumption of the Republic of Korea's public wastewater treatment facilities is 4,900 GWh, which accounts for 1% of total electricity consumption in the Republic of Korea.

Currently, wastewater treatment facilities are uniformly operated to attain the quality standard of the effluent water irrespective of the influent water quality. However, the quality of the influent water changes according to the weather, season, and time in which people are active. Therefore, by analyzing the quality of the influent water and the power usage patterns of the wastewater treatment facilities, it appears to be able to avoid power-load-peak-time through efficient operation. In addition, it is expected that the wastewater treatment facilities can be utilized as Demand Response (DR) resource through the development of operational scenario for DR. DR is that a consumer adjusts demand to avoid power load peak according to the amount of power supplied to the grid [1].

In this study, we describe the power measurement system, the power usage pattern analysis, and the power consumption prediction model of the wastewater treatment facility for the application of DR Service.

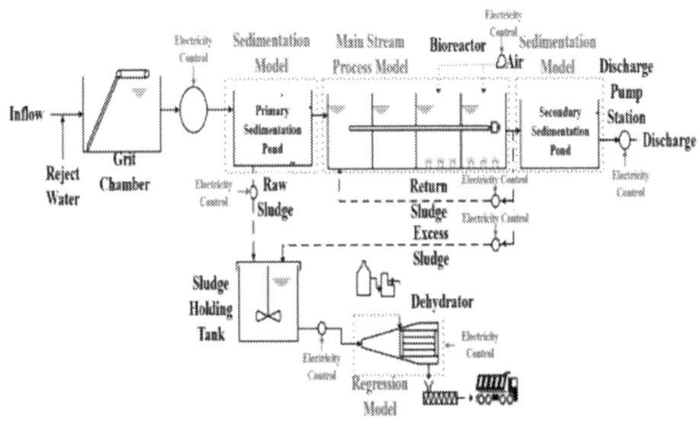

Figure 1. Flowchart of The Pilot System

II. CONSTRUCTION OF PILOT SYSTEM

Currently operated wastewater treatment facilities must ensure the quality of effluent water at the same time continuous inflow of wastewater, therefore it is impossible to change the experimental environment. Hence, we constructed the pilot system in order to analyze the changes of the quality of the effluent water and the power usage pattern of the processes due to changes in the quality of the influent water and operation scenario. The pilot system is that simplified the Sequencing Batch Reactor (SBR) process system. Figure 1 is a flowchart of the pilot system.

The SBR process consists in 6 steps such as Fill, Mix, React (Aerate, Mix), Settle, Decant, and Idle processes in one reactor and adjust the condition time according to the quality of the influent water [2].

In the Fill process, wastewater fills into the reactor and contacted with microorganisms. In the React process, organic and nutrient materials are removed by appropriate control of anaerobic, anoxic, and aerobic conditions through Mix and Aerate process. In the Settle process, separate the mixture into sludge and supernatant. In the Decant process, discharge the separated supernatant.

In order to apply DR service to the wastewater treatment facilities, it is necessary to analyze the power usage patterns of the individual devices and the overall power consumption measurement for the development of the operating scenario. The main devices of the pilot system used in this study are Influent Pump, Sludge Seeding Pump, Mixer, Submerged

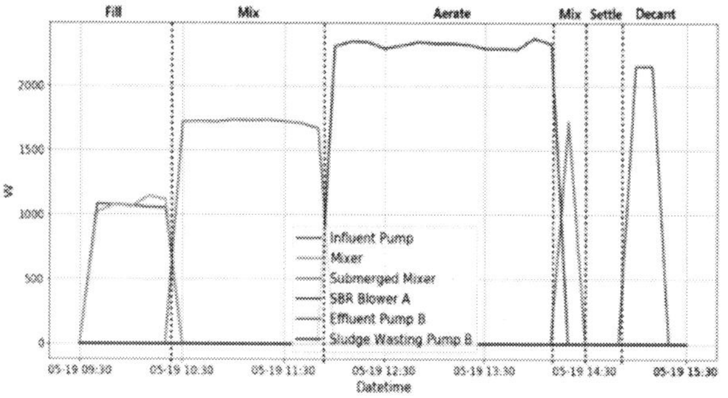

Figure 2. Power Usage Pattern of The Processes

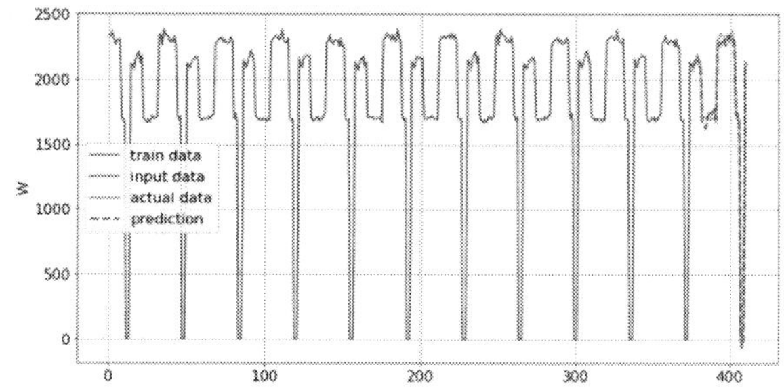

Figure 3. Train, Actual, and Predicted Data Pattern

Mixer, SBR Blower, Effluent Pump, and Sludge Wasting Pump. Therefore, we have developed a system that measures the total power consumption as well as the power usage of individual devices and stores them in a database. The power measurement system consists of the power meter, the gateway, and the server. In order to transmit and receive data wirelessly, the LoRa communication module is connected to a power meter installed in each device. The server receives the data through the LoRa Gateway and stores it in the database. The data includes voltage, current, power, and power factor.

III. Data Analysis and Model Design

The wastewater treatment process of the pilot system takes six hours in one cycle and proceeds in the order of Fill, Mix, Aerate, Mix, Settle and Decant process. Figure 2 shows the power usage patterns of the processes. There is no improvement point of efficiency in Fill and Decant Process because inflow and outflow of water must be fixed. However, Mix and Aerate process have a direct impact on the quality of the effluent water. In addition, the Mixer and SBR Blower used in the process can be variably controlled. Therefore, by controlling them variably according to the quality of influent water, it will be possible to reduce the power consumption and satisfy the effluent water quality standard.

In order to utilize the wastewater treatment facilities as DR resource, it is necessary to predict power consumption according to the influent water load and judge whether the effluent water quality standard and the power reduction amount can be satisfied through the variable control of the devices. In this study, we used the neural network model to apply features such as water quality and environmental factors in the future. The past power usage data of the pilot system is the result of the general wastewater treatment scenario. The data was measured in 10-minutes intervals and the unit is watts. Therefore, 36 data is stored in one cycle and 144 data is stored in one day. Based on this, we have constructed the neural network model that predicts one cycle (36 data) from past 24 hours data (144 data) [3]. The data looks like a time series. However, it showed poor performance when used in Recurrent Neural Network (RNN). Hence, we used Multi-Layer Perceptron (MLP) Model.

IV. Experiment and Evaluation

Figure 3 shows train data, actual data, and predicted data pattern. The left of the graph is the train and the input data pattern. The result of predict data by the model is on the right of the graph. The predicted data shows about 45.39 Root Mean Squared Error (RMSE) and about 1.79% Mean Absolute Percentage Error (MAPE). We confirmed that the predicted data is very similar to the actual data. Thus adding effluent water and influent water quality to the model will predict power consumption and effluent water quality depending on influent water quality.

V. Conclusion and Future Work

In this study, we have proposed the power measurement system, the power usage pattern analysis, and the power consumption prediction model of the wastewater treatment facility for the application of DR Service. The proposed system has collect power usage data from each device and predicts power usage pattern. The accuracy of the model in the experiments showed the feasibility of the proposed system. Adding the influent water quality and effluent water quality parameters to the model will enable the wastewater treatment facilities to be used as DR resource. For future research, we will add influent water quality and effluent water quality parameters to the model. We will then apply the model and system in large-scale wastewater treatment facilities and measure performance.

Acknowledgment

This work was supported by the Korea Institute of Energy Technology Evaluation and Planning (KETEP) and the Ministry of Trade, Industry & Energy (MOTIE) of the Republic of Korea (No. 20172010000780)

References

[1] M. H. Albadi and E. F. El-Sadany, "A summary of demand response in electricity markets," Electric power systems research, vol. 78, no. 11, pp. 1989-1996, 2008.

[2] S. Mace and J. Mata-Alvarez, "Utilization of SBR technology for wastewater treatment: an overview," Industrial & engineering chemistry research, vol. 41, no. 23, pp. 5539-5553, 2002.

[3] D. F. Specht, "A general regression neural network," IEEE transactions on neural networks, vol. 2, no. 6, pp. 568-576, 1991

Distributed Sensing System for an Old Vineyard in the Douro Demarcated Region - North Portugal

Sérgio Silva*†**, Salviano Soares*¶, Filipe Cabral Pinto§ Diogo Duarte‡, João Barroso*† and Justino Soares‖
*Engineering Department School of Sciences and Technology, UTAD, Vila Real, Portugal
**Globaltronic, Aveiro, Portugal
†INESC TEC -INESC Technology and Science Porto, Portugal
Email: sergio.s.silva@ inescporto.pt
‡Department of Electronics, Telecommunications and Informatics, UA, Aveiro, Portugal
§Altice Labs, Aveiro, Portugal
¶IEETA - UA, Aveiro, Portugal
‖Quinta do Crasto, Vila Real, Portugal

Abstract—**Two-thirds of the world's population currently lives in areas that experience water scarcity for at least one month every year. And like humans, plants, and especially grapes in vineyards, need the correct amount of water in order to grow healthy. Therefore, to assist the irrigation process, we do not only need to use reliable measuring systems to gauge the water amount per plant, but also to estimate the kg of chemical agents per hectare, like fertilisers, that contribute to the growing of the plants, as well as the pollution of rivers and water supplies. The implemented monitoring station is part of a Distributed Sensing System Model (DSS) that allows continuous measurements over time, and is based on an autonomous wireless sensor network capable of measuring the parameters of interest and storing all this information. The implemented station is fully autonomous, receiving energy from a solar panel that charges the two main batteries, even if there is no direct sunlight available. The station communicates to the remote sensors by RF and can be remotely accessed using 3G and Narrow Band IoT (NB-IoT). Besides the RF sensors, the station allows multiple interfaces to connect other sensors, as is the case of the developed sensor board that measures different gases like Nitrogen Dioxide (NO2) and Carbon Monoxide (CO) using I2C calibrated sensors for easy replacement and station adaptation. Traditional wind and rain sensors are supported, allowing new sensor value comparison and validation.**

Keywords-Weather Station; Sensors: Humidity, Temperature, CO, NO, CO2, O3, Dust, Pressure, Light, Anemometer; RF; LoRa; NB-IoT; GatewayFE; Old Vineyards; Quinta do Crasto.

I. INTRODUCTION

Agriculture is one of the most ancient activities of man, and a place where it is difficult to introduce innovation and technology due to the lack of investment and the difficulty to show the benefits of this introduction into productivity and profitability while minimizing unintended impacts on wildlife and the environment. Nevertheless, the use of information from the environment, especially when we speak about precision agriculture, has demonstrated that it is possible to maximize crop production while minimizing watering and fertilization schemes [1].

One of the biggest issues, when installing monitoring weather systems is the need of maintenance and station cost. An unattended wireless sensors network able to measure the parameters of interest like the amount of water in the soils, the Electrical Conductivity (EC - as a measure of total nutrients), soil thermal properties (temperature, thermal conductivity, heat capacity, and thermal diffusivity – as a measure of how energy is partitioned in the soil profile), water flux, and environmental temperature at the surface is one of the most promising technics developed by Valente in 2018 [2].

The developed sensor uses RF to connect to a main station that is fully energy autonomous, gathering energy from a solar panel that is stored into two main batteries, even if no direct Sun is available. Figure 1 shows the implementation of the data acquisition network.

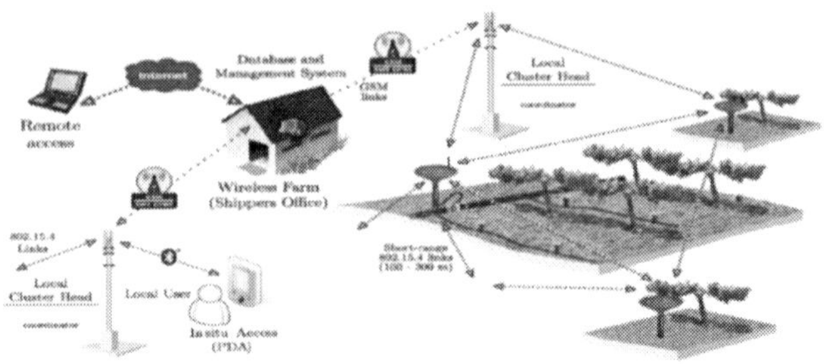

Figure 1. In-field data acquisition network.

This work presents a precision viticulture environment of "Quinta do Crasto", located in a prime spot in the Douro Demarcated Region in Northern Portugal. This region is characterized by the extreme weather condition and its own peculiar combination of topography, geology and water resources, all of which come together to form the unparalleled theatre of global winemaking. Quinta do Crasto soils are composed of schist complex types, and have been worked into steep slopes near the river in a remarkably awe-inspiring work of human ingenuity. The traditional "socalcos" (terraces with stone retaining walls) house the oldest vines, some dating more than one hundread years. An average of 5,000 plants/hectare of younger vines are planted vertically on slopes of less than 35%. On the slopes greater than 40%, "patamares" (more recent terraces) carry either one or two rows of vine, with a density of between 3,000 to 3,500 plants/hectare.

The excellent sun exposure with primarily eastern and southern aspects, in conjunction with the dry conditions of the Cima Corgo sub-region and the ability of schist soils to absorb and retain heat, come together to force the roots of these vines to grow dozens of meters deep in search of water. This also provides competition between the plants and contributes to the complexity and intensity of the wines produced.

The quality of these wines and this *terroir* also requires closely monitoring every step in the grape growing and wine-making process from pruning to harvest. Safeguarding the identity of vineyards is a fundamental prerequisite for the preservation of a unique genetic heritage and the only way to ensure the continuity of the old Douro vineyard, *Vinha Maria Teresa*, that give rise to internationally recognized wines [3].

In this complex scenario, a Distributed Sensing System can gather information that can help in understanding vineyard variability and therefore how it might be managed, thus improving the quantity and quality of the wines, not to mention ensuring the consistent production of the highest quality wines, year after year, in a matchless wine in their character and uniqueness.

Figure 2 shows the *terroir* of Quinta do Crasto.

Figure 2. *Vinha Maria Teresa*, Quinta do Crasto

In Section II, the objectives of the system are described, from the hardware and software perspective, to costs. The communication systems that were used are presented in Section III. In Section IV, the hardware implementation is exposed. In contrast, Section V presents the software implementation and the system web interface. Finally, Section VI presents the main conclusions and future work.

II. Objective

The primary objective of this work is to implement the hardware and firmware that will allow the Distributed Sensing System Model described in [4]. As stated, the system must be able to implement a Wireless Aboveground Sensor Network (WASN) capable of sensing and transporting data towards the central monitoring station [4], but with capacity to use different bands like 433 MHz and 868 MHz. The system should also be fully energetically autonomous, i.e., capable of harvesting energy from the nature.

The DSS platform must incorporate information from remote sensing, as well as *in situ* weather conditions, such as water source levels and soil history, and was stated that needed to be cost-effective, as less intrusive as possible, and include a reliable data communication system that allows data collection from sensors monitoring the crops, land, and environment. Towards these goals, a primary Gateway was developed using the latest technology available for communication and sensing. The hardware used for this implementation will be described in detail in the next chapter.

III. Comunication Systems

IoT services require connectivity to link objects to the Internet. Sensors and actuators require communication paths to allow exchanging information with cloud-based services, making possible the extraction of useful insights and also enabling the control of different connected infrastructures. Depending on the scenario, several options may be taken, from fixed to mobile, from ad-hoc to more structured networks. The "best" solution is always the one that fits to the customer needs and constrains. The application of IoT technology to an agricultural use case presupposes the existence of some requirements. It will be necessary to ensure wireless communications, at great distance and without waste of energy. These requirements map directly to the characteristics of Low Power Wide Area Networks (LPWAN).

There are already several commercial offers that make available similar solutions, that are able to cope with the diversity of applications requiring long range communications and reduced power consumption at lower costs. This variety of LPWAN systems can be roughly grouped in two major distinct sets: solutions using unlicensed radio bands and standardized systems operating under licensed spectrum.

The LoRa Alliance is an open association of companies targeting the specification of LPWAN for IoT applications. The members have detailed the open standard LoRaWan protocol in order to allow long range wireless IoT services for battery constrained devices [5] . It provides a secure bi-directional channel for communication between devices and applications supporting bit rates ranging from 0.3 kbps to 50 kbps, being the rate deeply dependent on the distance and the type of data to be sent. LoRaWan is built on top of the proprietary LoRa radio modulation technology from Semtech Corporation, which, however, relies on shared spectrum for radio communication.

3GPP has also developed efforts in the network specification for IoT, but operating under licensed spectrum. The systems were particularly simplified and new mechanisms were created to meet the specific needs of constrained devices. These efforts were particularly noticeable in the NB-IoT technology, which does not operate in the Long-Term Evolution (LTE) construct. NB-IoT was the main 4G solution to support ultra-low bit rate applications for limited devices communicating in large geographical areas. It is a cellular-based low power technology developed to support the link of low-cost devices to web-based applications [6]. It intends to reduce terminal costs and support extended coverage, while ensuring a long battery life. It supports communications up to 250 kbps on both directions with half-duplex operation using 180 kHz bands. The usage of licensed spectrum enables the full control of the communication channel making easier the availability of quality of service for IoT communications.

IV. Hardware

The sensors hardware is based on the Multi-Functional Probe (MFP), which is schematically represented in Figure 3. The MFP consists of one central heater needle and four surrounding thermistors, as reported by Mori et al. [8]. The needles are made from stainless steel tubing, 0.912 m min diameter, protruding 40 mm beyond the edge of the PVC mounting. Spacing between the heater and temperature sensors is about 8.5 mm. The heater was made from enameled Stablohm 800 A wire (0.062 mm in diameter and $440.8\,\Omega\,\mathrm{m}^{-1}$

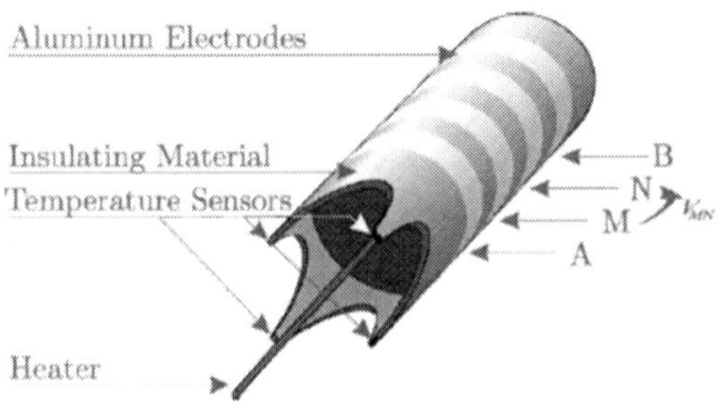

Figure 3. Multi-functional probe [7]

of resistivity) [9], which was inserted in the heater needle. The heater resistance was $100\,\Omega$ (heater resistivity of $2010\,\Omega\,\mathrm{m}^{-1}$). The needle is then filled with high thermal-conductivity epoxy glue, making it water-resistant, thus causing the heater to be electrically insulated.

The Wenner array is formed by four aluminum ring electrodes equally spaced with $3\,\mathrm{mm}$ separation [10]. The outer electrodes (denoted as A and B in Figure 3) provide for an alternated current source ($1\,\mathrm{mA}$ peak-to-peak and $100\,\mathrm{Hz}$ frequency), whereas the potential difference is measured across the two inner electrodes (M and N). The overall system, including battery, fits in a cylinder with $21.4\,\mathrm{mm}$ in diameter and approximately $50\,\mathrm{mm}$ long [4].

The developed Gateway, Figure 4, is based on WIIPIIDO, a powerful high-performance single-board computer equipped with a Quad-core ARM Cortex-A53 Processor@1.2 GHz and 2GB DDR3 memory RAM. The system offers four 16 Bit Analog to Digital Converter (ADC), an internal 8 GB INAND eMMC Flash Drive and four USB ports for expansion. The Real Time Clock Calendar (RTCC) and GPS provide the users with off the grid time and location keeping.

Figure 4. Gateway FE Plus

For connectivity, the Gateway offers several communication possibilities like Wi-Fi, Bluetooth, RF, GPRS and NB-IoT. The two RF Serial Peripherical Interface (SPI) modules implemented allow the Gateway to communicate on multiple bands and different protocols. A solar panel and the battery system allow energy harvesting with up to 3 days autonomy. The RTCC and Linux based system provide the database collection and system sensor monitoring.

There are also two relay Outputs and four digital inputs available. Figure 5 shows the schematics of the relay Outputs. The LED D9 is used to monitor the state of the output and it connects showing the user the relay activity. The output is used to automatically control the irrigation.

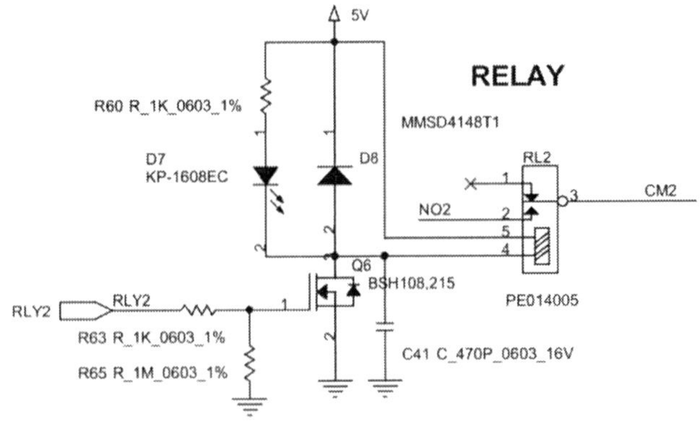

Figure 5. Schematic of the relay output

As for the inputs, they all are optically isolated as can been seen in Figure 6. For simplicity sake, only one of the Outputs and one of the Inputs were presented in the schematics. The inputs are used to allow manual control of the irrigation, as well as the detection of the pump activation, and the full level of the water tank.

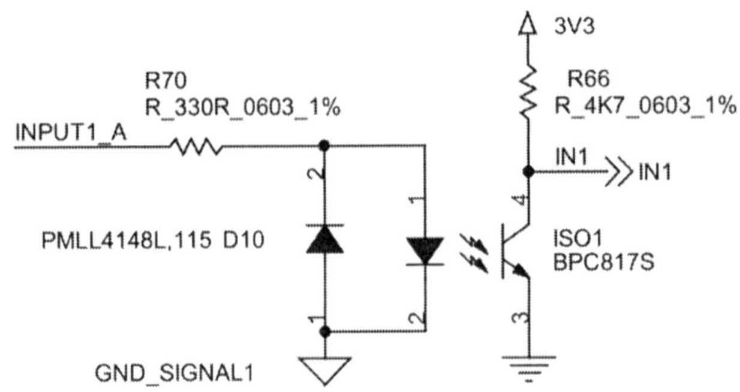

Figure 6. Schematic of the digital input

Due to the Douro Valley location, communication tends to be very difficult, so the Gateway allows remote communication through multiple backup systems like GPRS and Narrow Band IoT, with the latest being developed to enable efficient communication for wide geographical footprints. This module is based on the Sara N2.

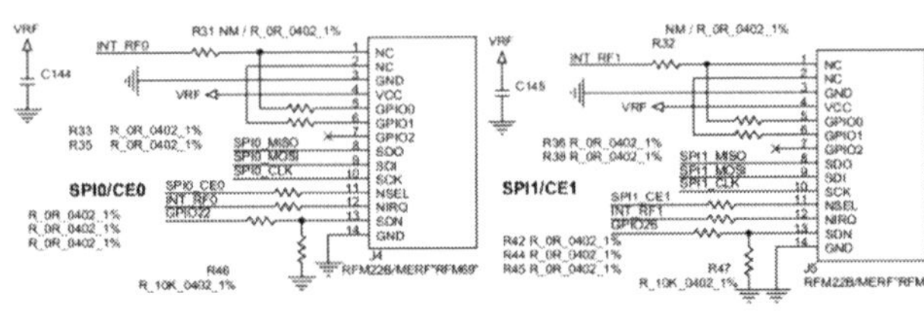

Figure 7. Schematic of RF module

The system communicates with the sensors using RF, and the schematic in Figure 7 shows one of the several RF modules implemented and supported by the Gateway. Up to two different modules can be used at the same time in the Gateway, allowing us to test different RF modules and their performance under the hillside vineyards in the Douro Region that is strongly conditioned by the original slope and relief of the parcels of vines.

To achieve maximum flexibility, the system should recharge its batteries using energy harvested from the surrounding environment, avoiding maintenance and human interference. Therefore, a solar panel and battery system were chosen for the task and they must be managed. The solar charger board was implemented using a PIC16F1938, as can be seen in the schematic represented in Figure 8. This board presents features such as battery charging, temperature control, battery discharging, light sensor, among others.

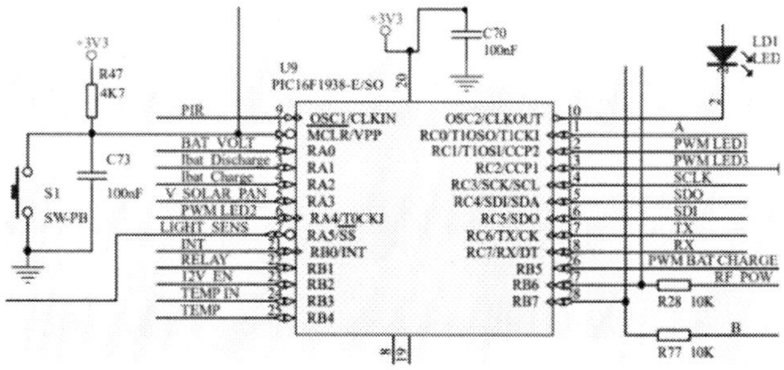

Figure 8. Schematic of Solar Charger

Besides the Gateway, the system also as a sensor board that allows the user to connect different sensors, from gas to the traditional weather station sensors like wind, rain, temperature and humidity. The board responsible to control the sensors communicates using RS-485 with the Gateway, and was implemented using the schematic in Figure 9.

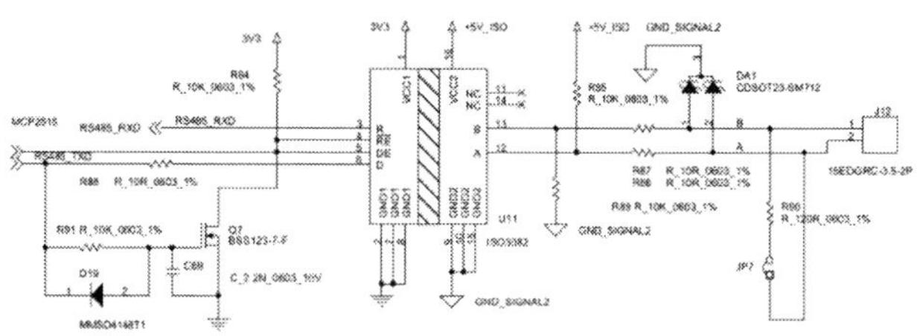

Figure 9. Schematic of RS-485

The ISO3082 transceiver was used since we need a good isolation, because it is expected that the I/O can be subjected to electrical noise transients from various sources, especially on the hillside where thunder storms tend to be more intense.

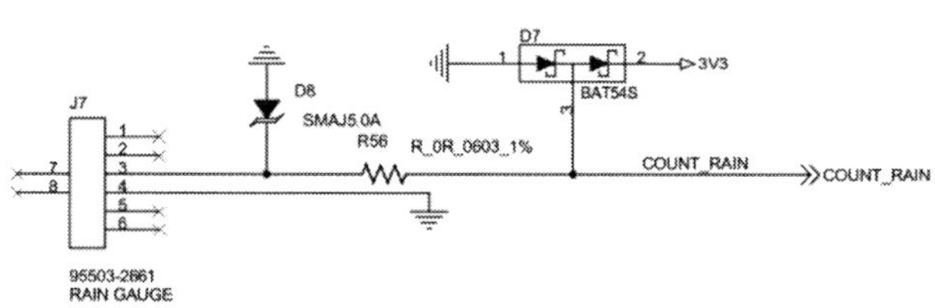

Figure 10. Schematic of the rain sensor

On the sensor board several traditional sensors can be connected, allowing the user to compare its values with the ones obtained from the new implemented sensors. The schematic

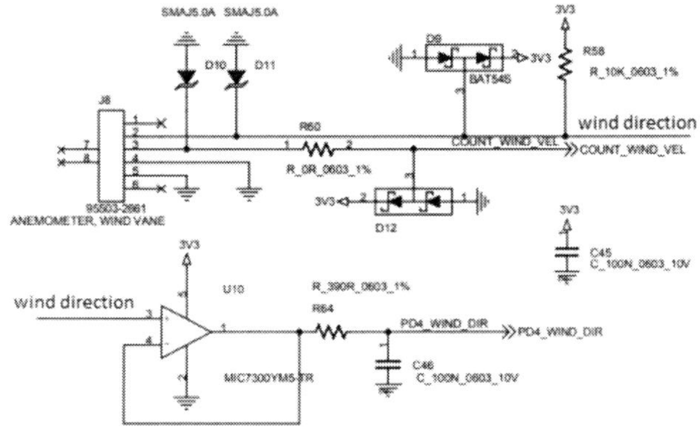

Figure 11. Schematic of the wind sensor

in Figure 10 shows the rain sensor connection. In the case of the wind sensor, the board implements the connection to an anemometer wind vane. Figure 11 shows this schematic implementation, which allows the user to detect not only the wind speed but also the wind direction.

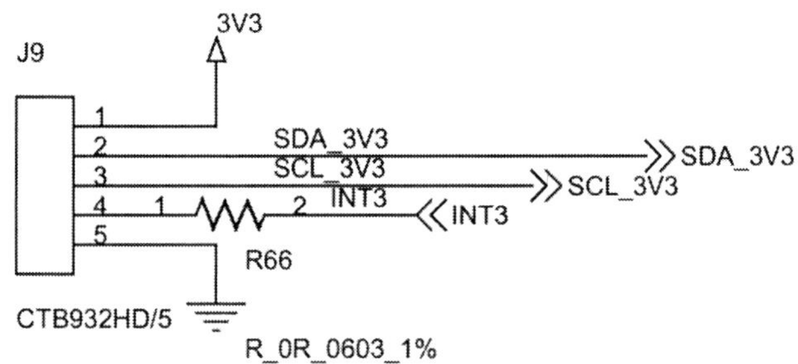

Figure 12. Schematic of the light and UV connector

The board allows light and UV measurements by using an Inter-Integrated Circuit (I2C) sensor. The connector schematic is showed in Figure 12. The sensor used is the Si1133, with a high accuracy UV Index Sensor and Ambient Light Sensor. In the schematic represented in Figure 13 we can see the sensor itself. The presence of the light diffuser allows the sensor to be inside a weather protection cover.

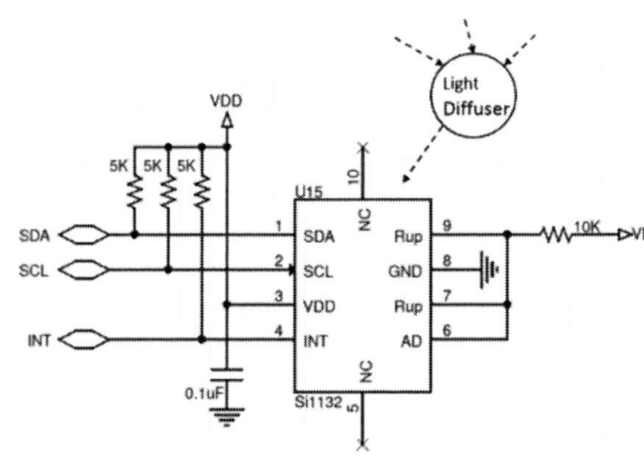

Figure 13. Schematic of the light and UV sensor

Besides the traditional sensors, the sensor board allows the connection of the following sensors, through I2C.

- CO - Carbon Monoxide: 2112B0052400 + 212B019900;
- NO - Nitric Oxide: 2112B0522400 + 212B019900;
- CO2 - Carbon Dioxide : MG-811;
- O3 - Ozone: MiCS-2614;
- DUST - Particulate Matter level : PPD42NS;
- PRESSURE - absolute pressure : LPS25HB;
- TEMP_HUM - Relative Humidity and temperature: Si7021-A20.

After connecting the sensors, the firmware automatically detects the type of sensor that was connected and starts sending the correspondent sensor data to the Gateway, which can be access using the available Wi-Fi connection. All data received from the sensors is stored in a database.

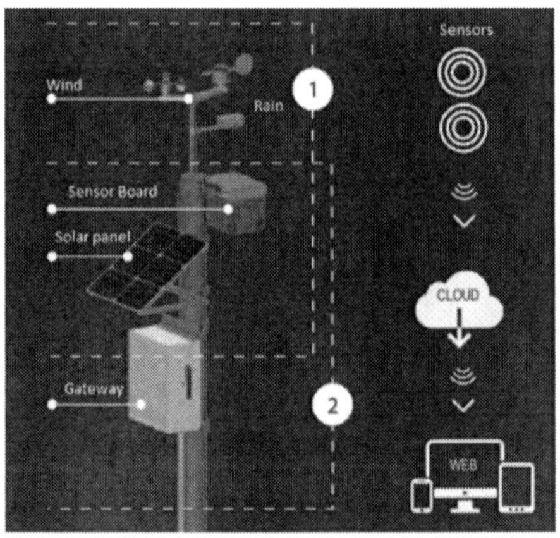

Figure 14. Main Pole configuration

Figure 14 shows the pole layout for the Gateway, Sensor Board, Solar Panel and traditional wind and rain sensors.

V. SOFTWARE

The software platform install was developed in JavaScript, under the NodeJS application platform over the Linux operating system. This makes the software platform independent, i.e., able to run under any device with a web browser install, thus highly scalable since the NodeJS is an asynchronous event driven JavaScript meaning that every network call creates a parallel process that handles the call without blocking the event-loop. This also implies that every callback function will work in parallel, but in a single thread.

Although at a first glanced the above does not seems important, the fact that there can be several users, and even sensors that will require access to the system and to the database at the same time can, on a networking environment, be problematic. The selected environment provides asynchronous operations avoiding blocking operation.

Figure 15 shows the opening page of the developed platform. On its left side, the sensors that have alarms, (for example battery below 50%) and on the right side the last time a sensor has communicated with the platform, along side

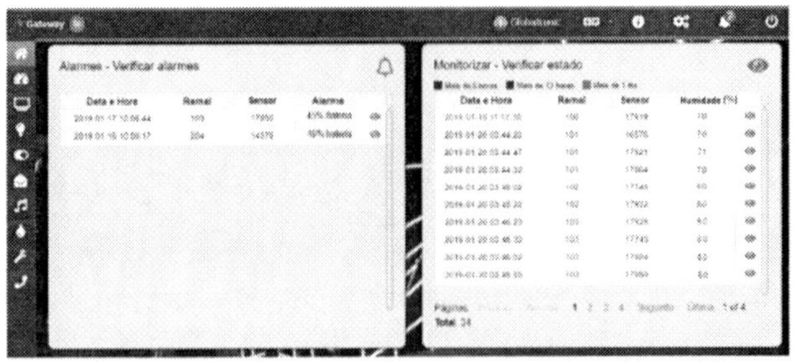

Figure 15. Main page of the developed platform

some meta-data, as well as the soil humidity % at the time of the message. All sensor data can be seen by pressing the correspondent sensor line. Figure 16 shows the sensor screen.

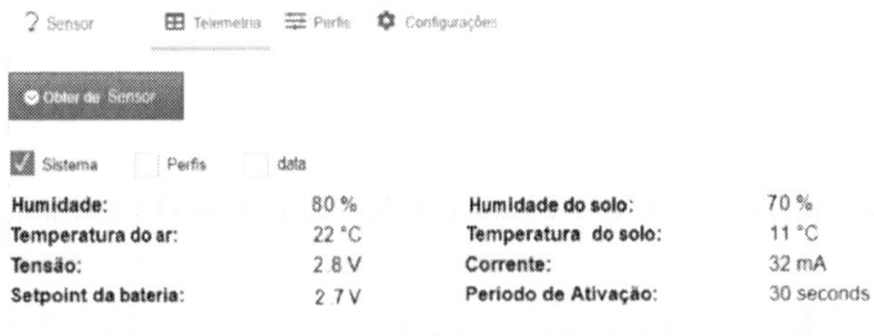

Figure 16. Sensor screen

The sensor has two additional screens: one for profile *Perfis* and the *Data* screen. The first allows sensor configuration, activation time and the amount of times the sensor activates during each day. The last shows all sensor data besides the one present on the system screen like thermal conductivity, heat capacity, and thermal diffusivity. In this phase, the system is mainly collecting data that will be analyzed and transformed into useful data. Besides sensor analysis and configuration, we can also configure users and their level of permissions or access, as seen in Figure 17.

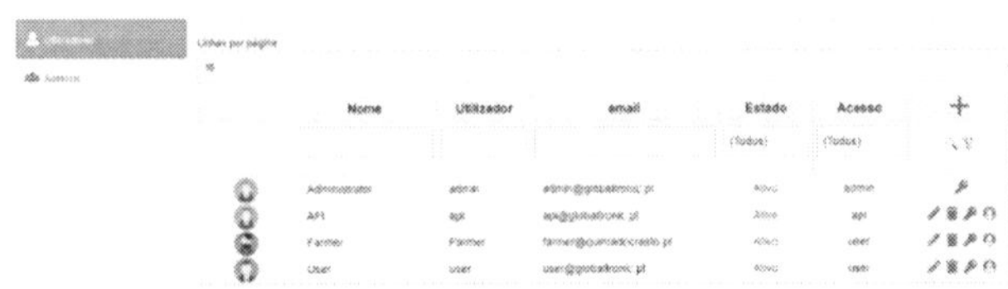

Figure 17. User configuration page

In page *Rega*, or Watering, the user can activate the watering system and control up to 18 different watering pumps, as well as configure the running and starting time for one or more pumps at the same time. Figure 18 illustrates this screen.

Finally, Figure 19 depicts the RF configuration, where it is possible to configure up to two different RF modules working simultaneously, allowing the user to test different bands, distances and protocols.

Another interesting screen refer is the Macro, since it grants users' the possibility to define sets of conditions that when realized, trigger an custom action. For example, if a sensor is below a certain Humidity %, then the correspondent pump

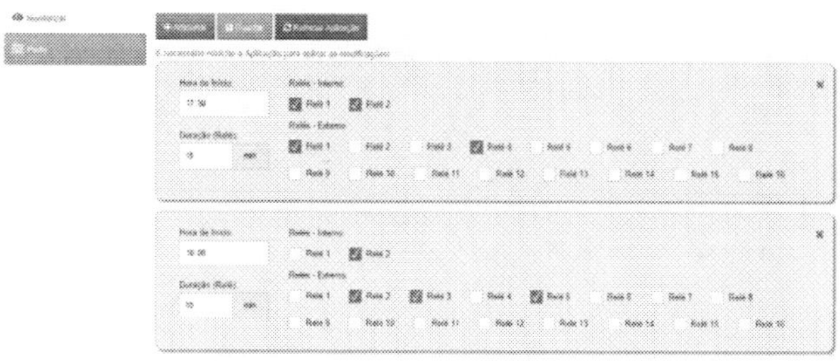

Figure 18. Watering configuration page

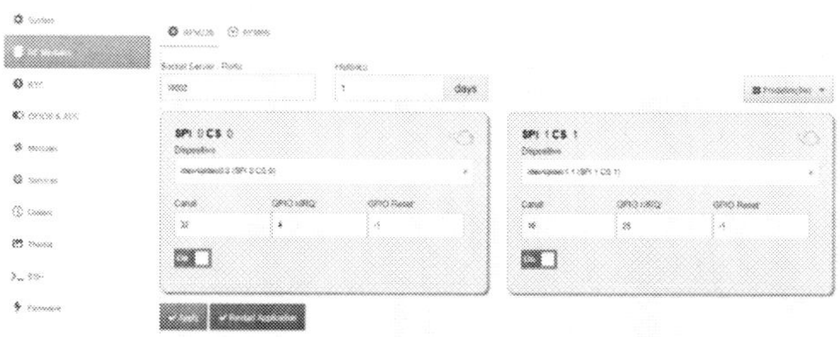

Figure 19. RF configuration page

will be triggered during a certain amount of time, or an email can be sent to the Farmer.

VI. Conclusion and Future Work

In this paper we have described the DSS system implemented at Quinta do Crasto. The described hardware and software provide the means to accomplish the objectives proposed by the author on his paper [4]. A state of art Gateway was implemented and described in detail, being fully autonomous and able to harvest energy from the nature.

The system can connect to the network using several methods, from Ethernet, 3G/4G, NB-IoT and Wi-Fi. On the other hand, users can connect to it using direct access point or through Bluetooth. Regarding sensors connectivity, besides the newly developed sensors, there is also the possibility to connect several traditional weather sensors, permitting comparison of values between both.

The DSS also implements several RF modules at the same time, allowing band comparison and protocol comparison in terms of reliability and message lost. Furthermore, through the implemented software and hardware, it is possible to use internal and external relays to control watering pumps. So, from the above, it is concluded that the system fully supports the defined requirements, with the next phase being real time, in-field testing.

Future works will pass through the implementation of the new sensors for wind, using ultrasounds, and rain, using sound. The data collected using the existing sensors will be analyzed and used for the DSS model implementation.

Acknowledgment

This work is financed by the ERDF European Regional Development Fund through the COMPETE Programme (operational programme for competitiveness) within project ref. POCI-01-0145-FEDER-006961 and by National Funds through the FCT Fundação para a Ciência e a Tecnologia (Portuguese Foundation for Science and Technology) within project ref. UID/EEA/50014/2013.

References

[1] R. R. Shamshiri, C. Weltzien, I. A. Hameed, I. J. Yule, T. E. Grift, S. K. Balasundram, L. Pitonakova, D. Ahmad, and G. Chowdhary, "Research and development in agricultural robotics: A perspective of digital farming," International Journal of Agricultural and Biological Engineering, vol. 11, no. 4, 2018, pp. 1–14.

[2] A. Valente, A. Saraiva, N. Ferreira, and S. Soares, "On the Design and Construction of Dual-Probe Heat-Pulse Soil Moisture Sensor: Towards an Industrial Solution," in ALLSENSORS, At Rome, Italy, 4 2018.

[3] Quinta do Crasto - Uma História que vem de longe (1615-2018), Dec. 2018, ISBN: 978-989-20-8980-5.

[4] S. Silva, S. Soares, A. Valente, and A. Moreira, "Distributed Sensing System Model for Future Internet Agricultural Application," in Proceedings PEECC 2015 - Doctoral Consortium, 2 2015.

[5] "Long Range Wide Area Network," 2019, URL: https://www.lora-alliance.org/ [accessed: 2019-01-16].

[6] M. Lauridsen, I. Z. Kovács, P. Mogensen, M. Sorensen, and S. Holst, "Coverage and Capacity Analysis of LTE-M and NB-IoT in a Rural Area," in Vehicular Technology Conference (VTC-Fall), 2016 IEEE 84th. IEEE, 2016, pp. 1–5.

[7] A. Valente, R. Morais, A. Tuli, J. W. Hopmans, and G. J. Kluitenberg, "Multi-functional probe for small-scale simultaneous measurements of soil thermal properties,water content, and electrical conductivity," Sensors and Actuators, A: Physical, 2006, pp. 70–77.

[8] Y. Mori, J. Hopmans, A. Mortensen, and G. Kluitenberg, "Multi-Functional Heat Pulse Probe for the Simultaneous Measurement of Soil Water Content, Solute Concentration, and Heat Transport Parameters," Vadoze Zone, vol. 2, 2003, pp. 561–571.

[9] N. Zhang, G. Fan, K. Lee, G. Kluitenberg, and T. Loughin, "Simultaneous measurement of soil water content and salinity using a frequency-response method," Soil Science Society of America, vol. 68, 2004, pp. 1515–1525.

[10] C. Donfack, "Caractérisation de contacts électrodes-tissus pour les stimulateurs neuro-musculaires implantables," Mémoire de maîtrise, École polytechnique de Montréal, Canada, 2000.

Evaluation of LP-WAN Technologies for Fire Forest Detection Systems

Daniel Adorno*, Salviano Soares†, José Lima‡, and Antonio Valente§

*University of Trás-os-Montes and Alto Douro
Vila Real, Portugal
Email: adornogomes@gmail.com

†IEETA - UA
and University of Trás-os-Montes and Alto Douro
Vila Real, Portugal
Email: salblues@utad.pt

‡INESC TEC - INESC Technology and Science
and Research Center in Digitalization and Intelligent,
Robotics, Polytechnic Institute of Bragança,
Bragança, Portugal
Email: jllima@ipb.pt

§INESC TEC - INESC Technology and Science
and University of Trás-os-Montes and Alto Douro,
Vila Real, Portugal
Email: avalente@utad.pt

***Abstract*—Low Power Wide Area Networks (LP-WAN) are receiving a lot of attention because of their ability to communicate using radio frequency in long distances, with low-power consumption and low-cost devices. In this paper, we provide a comparison between the two LP-WAN platforms that are leading the market, the Sigfox and the LoRaWAN, based on the literature. Both platforms are analyzed considering the context of the forest fire detection and verification systems. Many aspects are being considered to identify which LP-WAN is more adequate to be used in this kind of systems, such as battery lifetime, coverage range, business model and costs. The comparison shows that both platforms are very similar in most of the aspects, although LoRaWAN is more flexible than Sigfox on the deployment and management of the network infrastructure. LoRaWAN allows customers to implement and manage their own infrastructure network, which is essential in systems which monitor vast forest areas.**

Keywords–IoT; LoRaWAN; Sigfox; Fire detection.

I. INTRODUCTION

Forest is one of the most important resources of the earth that protects the ecological balance. It has a huge impact on reducing the emission of greenhouse gases, soil erosion, atmospheric carbon absorption, moderating the temperature, and regulating rainfall. A forest fire is considered one of the most dangerous natural accidents, caused by natural forces or human activities. It can affect practically all the forests in the world, having many consequences such as physical, biological and environmental [1]–[3]. In the last decade, with the advent of the Internet of Things (IoT), many forest fire detection and verification systems based on Wireless Sensor Network (WSN) technology were being proposed. In fact, these identified technologies represent an advance in comparison with traditional forest fire prevention [4]. But, most of those systems used short-range radio communication with mesh network protocols, and long-range communication based on Global System for Mobile Communications (GSM). In general, this approach contributes to an increase of the energy consumption and the cost of the system [5], [6].

Recently, a new concept of wireless telecommunication wide area network has arisen to attend the need to develop highly scalable systems with low-cost, low-power consumption, with the capacity to communicate in long distances using radio frequency [7]. Nowadays, there are many platforms and technologies based on this new paradigm called Low-Power Wide Area Networking (LP-WAN). In this article, we will compare two of those platforms, commercially available, that are leading the market: LoRa and Sigfox [8]. The goal is to identify which of them is more adequate to be used in forest fire detection and verification systems, as depicted in Figure 1. More specifically, this system should cover an area of $6600\,\mathrm{km}^2$, involving urban, rural and forest spaces (Figure 2, Bragança District, Portugal).

Besides Sigfox and LoRa being the most popular LP-WAN platforms, they were also chosen to be compared in this article because both operate in unlicensed bands, reducing the final cost of the solution [9]. Sigfox is a closed platform and LoRa is an open platform [6]. The two platforms are available for the customers as Network-as-a-Service (NaaS). But, LoRa allows customers to create their own infrastructure without the need to contract any service [10], [11].

The rest of the article is organized as follows: Section II presents the state of the art on LP-WAN technologies and platforms, section III describes the LoRaWAN and Sigfox low power wide area networks where the business model, the architecture, the technical aspects and the costs are stressed. Section IV performs

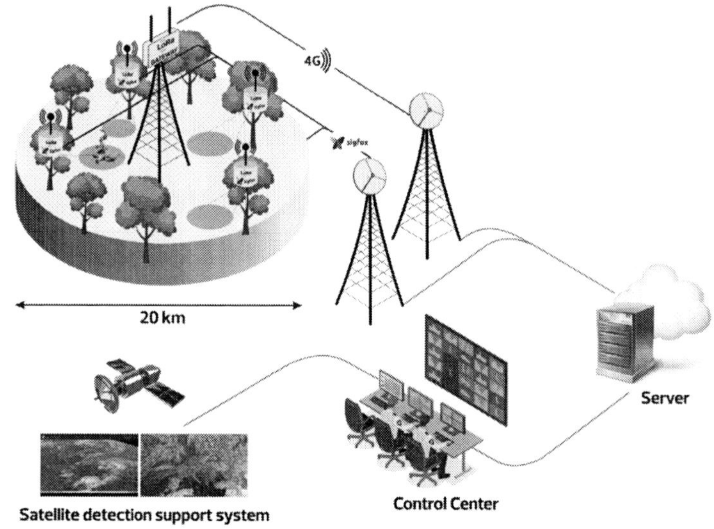

Figure 1. Overview

a comparison between the presented platforms. Conclusion is described in Section V.

Figure 2. Case study - Bragança, Portugal

II. RELATED WORK

Marco Centenaro *et al.* [6] make a presentation about the main characteristics of the LP-WAN paradigm, focusing on the platforms that operate in the unlicensed spectrum. They compares three platforms commercially available: LoRaWAN, Sigfox and Ingenu. These platforms are analyzed in terms of efficiency, effectiveness, and architectural design, especially for smart city applications. Also, they present practical results of experiments and deployments with IoT networks based on LoRaWAN, developed in the city of Padova, Italy. Raza *et al.* [7] presents the most important Low Power Wide Area (LPWA) platforms and technologies available in the market, the standardization activities developed by different standards organizations and the industrial consortia built around some LP-WAN technologies. They point that LP-WAN technologies have similar approaches, limitations and challenges. Also, they highlight the need for standards because of the variety of LP-WAN solutions which is resulting in a fragmented market. They provide an overview of many standardization efforts. Also, they make a comparison of the following LP-WAN platforms: LoRaWAN, Sigfox, Ingenu, Weightless-N and NB-IoT. The comparison is based on business and technical aspects. Sinha *et al.* [9] analyze and compare two LP-WAN platforms based on licensed and unlicensed bands, respectively, NB-IoT and LoRaWAN. They provide a survey on both technologies, describing the technical differences in terms of physical features, network architecture and MAC protocol. The comparison shows that LoRaWAN has advantages in terms of battery lifetime, capacity and cost. NB-IoT also has advantages , like QoS, latency, reliability and range. They consider application scenarios and show the current status of these technologies in Korea, Japan, and China. Mekki *et al.* [8] provide a comprehensive and comparative study of the three LP-WAN platforms that are competing for large-scale IoT deployment worldwide: Sigfox, LoRaWAN and NB-IoT. The first two, based on unlicensed bands, and the last one, on licensed bands. The platforms are compared, showing the technical differences between Sigfox, LoRaWAN and NB-IoT in terms of IoT success factors such as quality of service, coverage, range, latency, battery life, scalability, payload length, deployment and cost. The result of the comparison shows that Sigfox and LoRaWAN have advantages in terms of battery lifetime, capacity and cost. NB-IoT offers benefits in terms of latency and quality of service.

III. Sigfox and LoRa Platforms

This section addresses the business models, the architecture and the technical aspects for both Sigfox and LoRa low power wide area networks.

A. Business Model

Sigfox is a company and a LP-WAN network operator that commercializes its own IoT solution as Network and as a Service (NaaS) in around 57 countries. To cover all these countries, the company has partnership with various network operators. In the Sigfox's business model, customers can implement their own application in a fast and easy way, because they are only concerned about the end-devices. All the costs and management related to the infrastructure is Sigfox responsibility [10].

LoRa is a technology that was developed by a start-up called Cycleo in 2009. Three years later, Cycleo was purchased by Semtech, a company from USA. In 2015, LoRa was standardized by LoRa-Alliance that makes it an open software and IoT platform hardware. Furthermore, LoRa is deployed in around 100 countries. In LoRas business model, customers can use a public network offered by LP-WAN network operator (e.g., Orange in France, KPN in Netherlands, and Fastnet in South Africa), or create their own LoRa infrastructure. A network infrastructure based on LoRa can use hardware from many different manufacturers with a low cost [11].

B. Architecture

In terms of architecture, both platforms are very similar. Their architecture can be divided into four layers, as shown in Figure 3. In the first layer are presented the end-devices, which collect the monitored data. The end-devices send the collected data to the gateways or base stations, into the second layer. In the third layer, the network server receives the data from the gateways, process and stores the data into the databases. At the upper layer, the application layer the end-users access the information acquired by the end-devices, through specific applications, such as industrial monitoring, home automation, smart city applications, smart grid and smart metering applications. End-devices and gateways communicate using radio frequency. The Network layer communicates with the Gateway and Application layers using a TCP/IP based communication [10], [11].

TABLE I. LoRa end-devices classes

	Class A	Class B	Class C
Communication	Bidirectional	Bidirectional	Bidirectional
Power consumption	Low	Medium	High
Latency	High	Low	Low
Messages	Unicast	Unicast and Multicast	Unicast and Multicast

C. Technical aspects

Regarding the radiofrequency, both Sigfox and LoRa use unlicensed Industrial, Scientific and Medical (ISM) radio bands (868 MHz in Europe, 915 MHz in North America, 433 MHz in Asia)

At Sigfox network, the end-devices connect to the base-stations using Binary Phase-Shift Keying (BPSK) modulation in an ultra-narrow band sub-GHZ ISM band carrier. Sigfox supports bidirectional communication, uplink (from the end-device to the base station) and downlink (from the base station to the end-device). The number of messages over the uplink is limited to 140 messages per day, and the maximum payload length for each uplink message is 12 bytes. The number of messages over the downlink is limited to four messages per day. Sigfox permits encrypted messages using the the algorithm AES-128. Accordingly with the company, the communication is up to 30–50 km in rural areas and 3–10 km in urban areas [6], [10]. The battery lifetime for each end-device is around 8 years [7].

On the other hand, LoRa also supports a bidirectional communication but provided by the chirp spread spectrum (CSS) modulation. It uses six spreading factors (SF7 to SF12) to adapt the data rate and range trade off. The data rate is between 300 bps and 50 $kbps$. It depends on the spreading factor and on the channel bandwidth. The maximum payload length for each message is 243 bytes. The LoRaWAN communication protocol is used by the LoRa platform. In this protocol, each message transmitted by an end-device is received by all the base stations in the coverage range of the system. Messages can be encrypted using the algorithm AES-128b. The communication range is between 15–20 km in rural areas and between 3–5 km in urban areas. LoRaWAN considers three classes of end-devices as presented in Table I [11], [12]. The battery lifetime is around 10 years for each LoRa end-device [7].

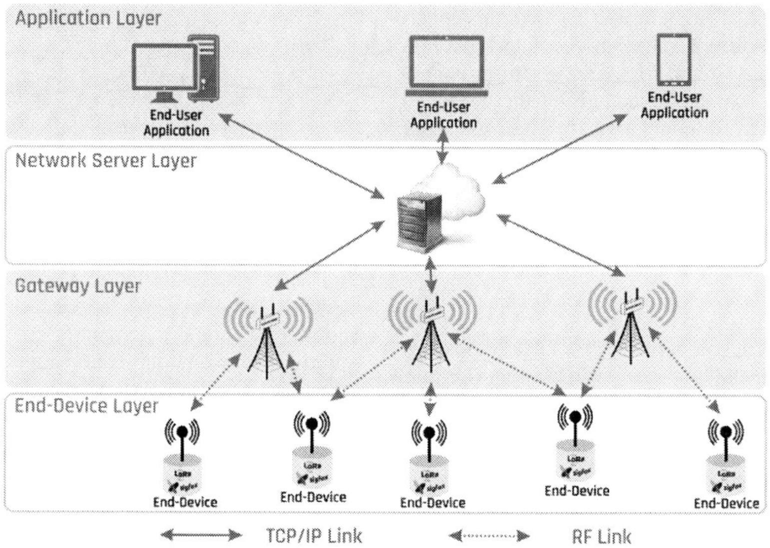

Figure 3. Lora and Sigfox architecture

TABLE II. COMPARISON OF SIGFOX AND LORA COSTS

	Spectrum cost	Network infrastructure cost	End-device cost
Sigfox	Free	Not Applicable (Network as a Service)	\$1–\$5
LoRa	Free	\$100–\$1000/gateway	\$1–\$5

D. Costs

For both platforms, is possible to find into the market, end-device hardware with low prices from \$1 to \$3, in average. The connectivity subscription per unit is around \$1 per year, when applicable. Besides these items, there are other cost aspects like spectrum and network infrastructure that impacts an implementation [8], [9]. Table II shows a comparison for these topics.

IV. COMPARING THE PLATFORMS

Some relevant aspects for an IoT project will be compared, considering the presented Sigfox and LoRa characteristics as show in Table 3. The compared characteristics are:

Implementation time:
Necessary time until to get the project on production;

Initial investiments:
Initial monetary resources to create the IoT infrastructure;

Adaptative Data Rate (ADR):
Configurations to adjust the size of the message, and control the coverage range of the devices impacting on the power consumption;

Uplink messages:
Messages sent from the end-devices to the network server;

Downlink messages:
Messages sent from the network server to the end-devices;

Maximum payload:
Maximum size of the uplink messages (in bytes);

Coverage and range of the gateways:
The maximum distance of communication between an end-device and a gateway in urban and rural areas.

In addition, other IoT comparison factors may be added [8]. These factors include the quality of service, battery life, latency, scalability, deployment and cost. The spider web diagram presented in Figure 4 summarizes the comparison between these factors for Sigfox and LoRaWAN low power wide area networks.

TABLE III. COMPARISON OF SIGFOX AND LORA

	LoRa	SigFox
Implementation time	Higher	Lower
Initial investiments	Higher	Lower
Adaptative Data Rate (ADR)	Yes	No
Uplink messages	Unlimited	140 per day
Downlink messages	Unlimited	4 per day
Maximum payload	243 bytes	12 bytes
Coverage and range of the gateways	15 – 20 Km (Rural) 3 – 5 Km (Urban)	30 – 50 Km (Rural) 3 – 10 Km (Urban)

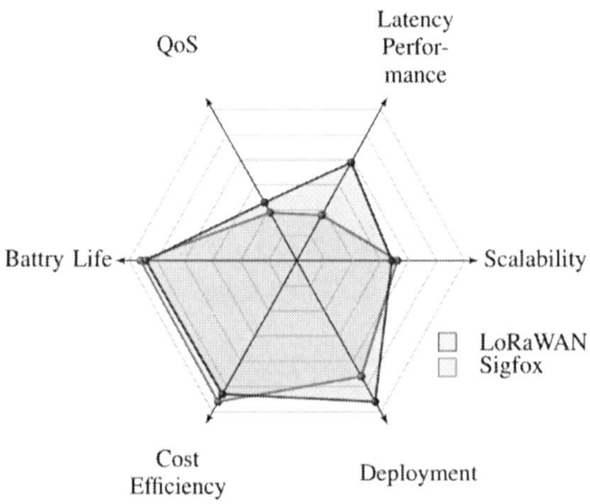

Figure 4. Spider web Diagram

V. CONCLUSION

This article analyzed and compared some aspects of LoRa and Sigfox low power wide area networks platforms. In all aspects, both platforms are very similar and could be used to implement forest fire detection and verification systems. However, Sigfox is limited in the regions of the world where the service is available. This is a great advantage showed by LoRa, because, if the system has to be implemented in a region where there is no LoRa public network available, the customers can implement their own networks. In terms of coverage, the considered area of the $6000\,\mathrm{km}^2$ could be covered by one or two LoRa base stations, based on the experience related in Belgium, where a LoRa network covers the entire country ($30\,500\,\mathrm{km}^2$) with seven base stations [9].

ACKNOWLEDGMENT

This work is financed by the ERDF European Regional Development Fund through the Operational Programme for Competitiveness and Internationalisation - COMPETE 2020 Programme within project "POCI- 01-0145-FEDER-006961", and by National Funds through the FCT - Fundação para a Ciência e a Tecnologia (Portuguese Foundation for Science and Technology) as part of project UID/EEA/50014/2013. This research was also partially supported by SAFe Project through PROMOVE - La Caixa.

REFERENCES

[1] J. Zhang, W. li, N. Han, and J. Kan, "Forest fire detection system based on zigbee wireless sensor network," Front. Forestry China, vol. 3, 09 2008, pp. 369–374.

[2] J. Zhang, W. Li, Z. Yin, S. Liu, and X. Guo, "Forest fire detection system based on wireless sensor network," 06 2009, pp. 520–523.

[3] L. Guang-Hui, Z. Jun, and W. Zhi, "Research on forest fire detection based on wireless sensor network," in 2006 6th World Congress on Intelligent Control and Automation, 01 2006, pp. 275–279.

[4] G. Kaur and M. Manshahia, "Wireless sensor networks for fire detection and control," International Journal on Future Revolution in Computer Science & Communication Engineering, 12 2017, pp. 14–21.

[5] R. Sanchez-Iborra and M.-D. Cano, "State of the art in lp-wan solutions for industrial iot services," Sensors, vol. 16, no. 5, 2016. [Online]. Available: http://www.mdpi.com/1424-8220/16/5/708

[6] M. Centenaro, L. Vangelista, A. Zanella, and M. Zorzi, "Long-range communications in unlicensed bands: the rising stars in the iot and smart city scenarios," IEEE Wireless Communications, vol. 23, 10 2015, pp. 60–67.

[7] U. Raza, P. Kulkarni, and M. Sooriyabandara, "Low power wide area networks: An overview," IEEE Communications Surveys & Tutorials, 01 2017.

[8] K. Mekki, E. Bajic, F. Chaxel, and F. Meyer, "A comparative study of lpwan technologies for large-scale iot deployment," ICT Express, 2018, in Press.

[9] R. S. Sinha, Y. Wei, and S.-H. Hwang, "A survey on lpwa technology: Lora and nb-iot," ICT Express, vol. 3, no. 1, 2017, pp. 14–21.

[10] "Sigfox world coverage, pricing and technical information," 2019, URL: http://www.sigfox.com/en/coverage/ [retrieved: February, 2019].

[11] "LoRa world coverage, pricing and technical information," 2019, URL: http://www.lora-alliance.org/ [retrieved: February, 2019].

[12] J. de Carvalho Silva, J. Rodrigues, A. Alberti, P. oli, and A. Aquino, "Lorawan - a low power wan protocol for internet of things: a review and opportunities," in 2017 2nd International Multidisciplinary Conference on Computer and Energy Science (SpliTech), 07 2017, pp. 1–6.

International Academy, Research,
and Industry Association (IARIA)
412 Derby Way
Wilmington, DE 19810

ISBN 978-1-5108-8360-4

CURRAN ASSOCIATES INC.
proceedings.com

International Journal on Advances in Security

2016 Volume 9 Number 3&4

ISSN: 1942-2636

IARIA